FAST & EASY FIVE-INGREDIENT RECIPES

FAST & EASY

FIVE-INGREDIENT RECIPES

A COOKBOOK FOR BUSY PEOPLE

PHILIA KELNHOFER

The Countryman Press
A division of W. W. Norton & Company
Independent Publishers Since 1923

DEDICATION

In "five-ingredient" style I wish to dedicate this book to:

1. All the busy people out there—I am one of you; life can be crazy busy. This book is dedicated to helping with mealtime inspiration and making your life a little easier.

2. My husband—my one true love. I love you more than I could ever possibly express. Thank you for your unwavering support and endless encouragement and for being the best taste tester and hand model this foodie girl could ever dream of.

3. My family and friends—thank you for everything. This book was originally going to be called "Five Ingredients with Friends and Family" because you are where it all started; you are the best. Thank you to my parents who taught me how to cook and that when you put your mind to something, you can achieve it. And to my father-in-law—a special thank-you to you for reading every single word in this book before I was ready to share it with the world.

4. The dedicated *Five Ingredient Friday* followers—your following of the series on my blog (www.sweetphi.com) is what allowed me to start this journey of creating a cookbook.

5. The entire team at the Countryman Press—thank you for turning my vision for this book into a reality and believing in my cookbook dreams.

Cooking well doesn't mean cooking fancy. —Julia Child

ACKNOWLEDGMENTS

They say it takes a village, and I can attest to that. This book would simply not have happened if it weren't for the entire village that has helped me. A few special thank-yous, however, are deserved.

To my husband, a million, no, a bazillion, thank-yous would never come close to enough. While some may think being the husband of a food blogger is 24/7 deliciousness, I know there are parts of the role that the world never sees: the endless boxes of "stuff" having to be broken down for recycling (I know I leave trash in the boxes; I'm the worst), the hundreds (more like thousands) of food photography props that need to be carried up and down from the basement because of space constraints, and the dishes—they are endless! Thank you for making my life so much better. You make me smile. You make my heart happy. I love you.

To Lynn, there is no one more fiercely loyal than you, I'm so glad to have you in my corner. You are simply the best and I love you. Our constant calls and texts keep me going, even when the going gets tough. All I have to do is think of the fact that "I hear it's really nice in Montana this time of year" and I smile. We should really go someday. And your famous line "as a professional courtesy" gets me every time.

To Jodie, you have always believed in me. From the first day we met, you have made me think if I wanted, I could. Thank you for your continuous support and encouragement; I love you.

To Meg, thank you for helping me think of creative ways to share my cookbook with the world! This world is such a small one, and I'm so happy we were able to connect.

To my editor, Ann, thank you for pointing out my love of exclamations! And thank you for making this book a success—turning *Five Ingredient Fridays* into a cookbook will forever make me grateful to you.

Most important, thanks to all of you for buying this cookbook! I love seeing all the #sweetphiblog sharing on social media; let's keep in touch and interact.

CONTENTS

INTRODUCTION

Sometimes after a busy day, the last thing you want to do is spend hours upon hours in the kitchen, cooking a recipe that involves a mile-long ingredients list. I'm right there with you. My name is Philia, Phi for short, and I'm here to help make dinnertime a little easier through fast and easy recipes.

Like you, I know a little something about being busy.

I work full-time, run a food blog (www.sweetphi.com), have a never-ending to-do list, and have a husband and family and friends I want to spend time with.

Dinnertime can be daunting. But it doesn't have to be. Whether for weeknight meals or last-minute dinner parties, I'm going to show you how five-ingredient recipes will save you time and money . . . and they're delicious, too.

A few years ago on a Friday night, I was having a conversation with one of my younger sisters who was in college at the time. She mentioned that while she loved cooking, she was really drawn to the simpler recipes I was creating. Recipes with few ingredients that she could pick up at her local grocery store and that offered amazing results.

Since it was a Friday evening I joked, "How about I start a 'Five-Ingredient Fridays' series?" She, along with everyone else I told, loved the idea and a new blog series was born.

Friday became the day I looked forward to, not only because of the upcoming weekend, but because I would share a recipe with five ingredients or less (water, salt and pepper, and cooking spray are not included in the count because chances are you have those in your kitchen . . . somewhere). I received such a positive response from readers writing to tell me that they had made a delicious meal for their families, and how shocked they were that all they used were five ingredients. Or, when I'd make a dish for friends, they'd say, "This has only five ingredients? Are you sure?" Yup, I'm positive.

Five ingredients is all it takes to create fantastic dishes.

Whether it's throwing together a quick dip or having some cookies ready to go from the freezer, I love simple recipes. Recipes that have amazing flavors, that don't take hours upon hours to make, and that have ingredients one can pronounce.

Simple, good food.

That is what cooking is all about for me: bringing friends and family together and showing home cooks that delicious food doesn't have to have a bazillion ingredients or take hours to make.

Creating this cookbook has been something I've wanted to do for years and the topic of easy recipes is one I'm super passionate about. I have a cookbook collection that is larger than I care to admit. I love discovering new ideas and gathering inspiration and looking at pictures—pictures are a must. If a cookbook doesn't have photographs, I find myself getting a little discouraged. I like having an idea of how the finished dish will look, so with each recipe I've included a photo for you. As someone once told me, "Cookbooks are my favorite books to read; you always know the ending."

That's not to say your interpretation of the recipes should be the exact same. You like things with a little more salt? Add an extra pinch. You like things with a little more kick? By all means, add that ghost pepper (eep . . . don't forget to tell your guests)!

Recipes are meant as a guide—a road map—to your kitchen adventures, of which I hope you have many.

In this cookbook, you will find 105 five-ingredient recipes, all accompanied by big, beautiful pictures.

I hope you enjoy,

Phi

BREAKFAST
AND
BRUNCH

BANANA COCONUT MUFFINS

Bananas
Sugar
Coconut Milk
Flour
Shredded Coconut

MAKES 12 MUFFINS

I love these muffins; they taste like banana bread but with added notes of coconut deliciousness. They're dense in both flavor and texture and are sweet but not too sweet. Plus, muffins are such a great breakfast food for when you're on the go, because they're portable. Make a batch, enjoy one, and freeze the rest for breakfasts during the week.

---

2 medium ripe bananas, mashed (see note)
½ cup sugar, plus 1 tablespoon for sprinkling
½ cup light coconut milk
1½ cups all-purpose flour
½ cup unsweetened shredded coconut, plus 1 tablespoon for sprinkling

---

NOTE

I like freezing ripe bananas so that whenever I want to make a batch of muffins, I can just remove them from the freezer and don't have to wait days for fresh ones to ripen. To freeze ripe bananas, wait until they are speckled brown, then peel and slice them in half, wrap in plastic wrap or put in a resealable plastic freezer bag, and label "ripe bananas: mm/dd/yy" so you know the date you froze them. Ripe bananas keep frozen for up to one year. To thaw, simply remove them from the freezer about an hour before you want to use them, and drain off any excess liquid.

1. Preheat the oven to 350°F. Line a muffin pan with 12 muffin liners and set aside.

2. With a hand mixer, in a large bowl, blend the bananas and ½ cup of the sugar on medium speed for 1 minute, then add the coconut milk and mix until combined. Add the flour and ½ cup of the shredded coconut and beat for 30 seconds, or until well combined (you don't want to overblend, so a few little clumps are okay).

3. Divide the batter among the lined muffin cups and sprinkle with a pinch each of sugar and shredded coconut (or use more or less sugar and coconut, as desired).

4. Bake the muffins for 40 to 45 minutes, or until they start to turn golden brown on top. Allow to cool for 5 to 10 minutes in the tins, then enjoy warm; or allow to cool completely and freeze for later enjoyment.

BUTTERMILK PANCAKES

MAKES 8 PANCAKES; SERVES 2 OR 3

Pancakes—one of the most quintessential American breakfast foods. These buttermilk pancakes are super easy to make and are everything a pancake should be—fluffy and delicious!

1 cup all-purpose flour
¼ cup sugar
1½ teaspoons baking soda
1 large egg
1 cup buttermilk
Cooking spray

NOTE

By using a cookie scoop, you get same-size pancakes. A ladle would also work.

1. Heat a griddle or nonstick skillet over high heat.

2. In a bowl, combine the flour, sugar, and baking soda and mix.

3. Make a well in the center (just indent with the back of your mixing spoon) and crack the egg into the well. Pour the buttermilk on top of the egg, stir from the center to break the egg yolk, and continue to stir until only a few small clumps are left (a few small clumps are okay; don't overmix).

4. Spray the griddle with cooking spray. With a 2-tablespoon cookie scoop or a spoon (see note), scoop about 2 table-spoons of pancake batter and pour onto the griddle. Cook for about 4 minutes on one side and then flip and cook for another 1 to 2 minutes.

5. Repeat until all the pancakes are made, then serve warm.

FRENCH TOAST CASSEROLE

Cinnamon Swirl Bread

Milk

Eggs

Brown Sugar

Sugar

SERVES 8 TO 10

Whenever we have friends staying over or are hosting a brunch, this is the dish I make. This French toast casserole is everything you could possibly hope for out of a brunch menu item—sweet, with a little bit of crunch from the caramelized sugar, and very comforting. It's definitely a crowd-pleaser.

1 loaf raisin cinnamon swirl bread
1 cup milk (I use 2% milk, but feel free to use whatever milk you have on hand)
5 large eggs
½ cup light brown sugar
½ cup sugar

NOTE
This casserole goes great with some bacon or breakfast sausage as a side.

1. Preheat the oven to 370°F. Spray a 9 x 13-inch baking dish with cooking spray.

2. Cut the bread into large chunks (I simply cut the entire loaf into sixths) and place the bread chunks in the prepared baking dish.

3. In a large bowl, whisk together the milk and eggs and pour on top of the bread pieces.

4. Sprinkle both sugars over the bread mixture.

5. Bake for 30 minutes, remove from the oven and allow to cool for 5 to 10 minutes, and serve.

Piecrust
Strawberry Preserves
Powdered Sugar
Milk
Sanding Sugar

HOMEMADE HAND PIES

MAKES 6 HAND PIES

After having your first homemade hand pie, you'll wonder where these were all your life and throughout your childhood. The flaky crust and warm fruity center are like no other. They can be made with whatever jam you have on hand, and if you don't want an extra-sweet breakfast, you can skip the glaze—although the sweet topping is the best part.

1 box refrigerated piecrust (2 ready-to-bake 9-inch crusts)
½ cup strawberry preserves or fruit spread

FOR THE GLAZE (SEE NOTES):
⅔ cup powdered sugar
1 tablespoon milk
1 to 2 tablespoons sanding sugar

NOTES

These pies are delicious for breakfast but can also be served as a dessert. If you don't want to add extra sugar by making a glaze, you could brush the sealed pies with an egg wash (1 large egg yolk beaten with ½ teaspoon of water), and sprinkle with some sanding sugar before baking.

1. Preheat the oven to 425°F. Line a baking sheet with parchment paper or a silicone baking mat and set aside.

2. Unroll one of the piecrusts on a large cutting board and cut the edges off the dough so that it resembles a large rectangle. Cut the piecrust down the middle and then into thirds, to form six rectangles. Repeat with the second piecrust so that you have 12 same-size dough rectangles.

3. Place 1 to 2 tablespoons of jam in the center of one of the rectangles and top with another rectangle of piecrust. Crimp all four edges with a fork (just press a fork around the edges, about ½ inch in). I also pinch the edges to make sure they're really sealed together (you don't want jam oozing out the sides).

4. Repeat until all the piecrust rectangles are used (you will have six sealed hand pies).

5. Place the pies on the prepared baking sheet and bake for 10 minutes, or until slightly browned around the edges. Remove from the oven and allow to cool for 5 minutes.

6. **While the pies are baking, make the glaze:** In a bowl, whisk together the powdered sugar and milk to make a smooth yet thick frosting—it should be easily spreadable. If the glaze is too thick, add a little more milk. If the glaze is too runny, add a little more powdered sugar.

7. Spoon the glaze onto the pies, sprinkle with some sanding sugar, and serve.

8. Leftover pies can be stored in an airtight container. To serve warm, reheat in the microwave on HIGH for 30 seconds.

HONEY BISCUITS

**Flour
Baking Powder
Butter
Buttermilk
Honey**

MAKES 6 BISCUITS

When I was living in North Carolina, I had my first biscuit for breakfast—a life-changing event for this girl who grew up in the Midwest. Although I've had many variations of biscuits, these slightly sweet honey biscuits with a beautiful buttery flavor are my favorite. Another thing I love about these biscuits is that they only take mere minutes to put together before baking.

**2 cups all-purpose flour, plus
2 tablespoons for dusting**
1 tablespoon baking powder
1 teaspoon salt
**4 tablespoons cold unsalted
butter, cut into pieces, plus
1 tablespoon, melted, for
topping**
¾ cup buttermilk
2 tablespoons honey

NOTES
To keep the butter cold, you could put it in the freezer for 5 minutes before handling it. I like to serve these biscuits with some butter and honey, or with some thinly sliced ham and make them into little biscuit sandwiches.

1. Preheat the oven to 350°F. Line a baking sheet with parchment paper or a silicone baking mat and set aside.

2. In a food processor, combine the flour, baking powder, and salt, process for 1 second, then add the cold butter pieces and process for 5 seconds, or until the butter is pea size and no larger chunks remain. Alternatively, if you don't have a food processor, you could cut the butter into the flour mixture.

3. Pour the flour mixture into a bowl, then pour in the buttermilk and honey. Stir with a wooden spoon and then knead with your hands for 30 seconds (the ingredients should combine to form a doughy mass, but don't overknead the dough or else it will result in dense biscuits). It will seem as if there is not enough liquid, but there is (if the dough is really not coming together, you can add a teaspoon or two more of buttermilk; alternatively, if the dough is too wet, you can add a teaspoon or two of flour).

4. Transfer the dough to a floured surface and, using your hands, flatten it into a ½-inch disk.

5. With a biscuit cutter, cut out six biscuits and place them on the prepared baking sheet. Brush the tablespoon of melted butter onto the biscuits. Bake for 18 to 20 minutes, or until golden brown. Remove from the oven, allow to cool for a few minutes, and serve and enjoy.

Oats
Milk
Vanilla Extract
Brown Sugar
Chocolate Chips

CHOCOLATE CHIP OATMEAL

MAKES 1 SERVING (RECIPE MULTIPLIES EASILY)

Oatmeal tends to get a bad reputation of being boring and bland, but with these ingredients it tastes like chocolate chip cookie dough oatmeal, something definitely not boring. Plus, when you're looking for a superquick breakfast, there's nothing that beats oatmeal that has a two-minute cooking time.

½ cup quick-cooking oats

1 cup low-fat milk, or coconut or almond milk

½ teaspoon pure vanilla extract

1 tablespoon light brown sugar

2 tablespoons semisweet chocolate chips

1. Combine the oats, milk, and vanilla in a tall, microwave-safe bowl (the oatmeal will rise while cooking) and stir a few times.

2. Microwave on HIGH for 2 minutes.

3. Remove from the microwave and stir in the brown sugar, and then sprinkle the chocolate chips on top and serve.

CHOCOLATE-COVERED BANANA SMOOTHIE

Chocolate Chips
Milk
Bananas
Vanilla Yogurt
Oats

SERVES 2

Have you ever had a chocolate-covered banana frozen treat? This smoothie tastes like that, but better, and is a totally delicious breakfast smoothie. Little chunks of the fudgy ganache flows through the straw when you're drinking this smoothie and you get to scrape the glass clean. I could have this smoothie for breakfast or for a dessert treat, it's so good.

1½ ounces semisweet chocolate chips (about ¼ cup)
1½ cups plus 2 tablespoons milk, divided
2 bananas, frozen (see note)
½ cup vanilla yogurt
½ cup quick-cooking oats

NOTE

The night before making this recipe, freeze the bananas. Peel, cut into 1-inch pieces, wrap in plastic wrap or place in a little resealable plastic bag, and freeze overnight.

1. In a small bowl, combine the chocolate chips and 2 tablespoons of the milk and microwave on HIGH for 30 seconds, then remove from the microwave and stir until smooth. Allow to cool slightly while you make the smoothie. Before serving the smoothie, spoon the chocolate ganache around the top rim of two glasses so that it drips down the insides.

2. In a blender, combine the remaining 1½ cups of milk and the frozen bananas, vanilla yogurt, and oats. Blend until smooth, 1 minute.

3. Pour the smoothie into the chocolate-coated glasses and serve (best served with a straw).

FREEZER BREAKFAST SANDWICHES

MAKES 4 BREAKFAST SANDWICHES

In a hurry most mornings? So am I! During the morning hustle and bustle, I sometimes don't have more than a few minutes to spare (if that), and so having breakfast sandwiches in the freezer solves the breakfast question. These sandwiches are super convenient; they only take a few minutes to warm up, so you'll have breakfast in a flash.

4 English muffins (I like to use whole wheat or multigrain; see note)
6 slices uncooked bacon
1 tablespoon unsalted butter
4 large eggs
¼ teaspoon salt
4 slices pepper jack cheese (see note)

NOTES
These sandwiches taste great on multigrain English muffins, but any bread you have on hand will work. I like to use pepper Jack cheese because it gives the sandwich a little flavor kick, but Cheddar or American cheese also work well. The sandwiches will keep in the freezer for up to 2 months.

1. Toast the English muffins and set aside. Line a large plate with three layered pieces of paper towel, place the bacon slices on the paper towel, and place two additional pieces of paper towel on top of the bacon. Microwave on HIGH for 3 minutes, then check for doneness and microwave in 30-second intervals until the desired level is reached. (I like crispy bacon, so I usually microwave it for 4 to 5 minutes total, or two to four extra intervals of heating.)

2. In a medium skillet over medium-high heat, melt the butter, then crack the eggs into the pan and loosely stir them around to break the yolks. Scramble them, sprinkle in the salt, then let them cook, without stirring, for 3 minutes. Remove from the heat. With a spatula, cut the eggs into four wedges, as you would slice a pie into quarters.

3. To assemble the sandwiches, place a piece of cheese on the bottom half of an English muffin, top with one-quarter of the eggs and 1½ slices of bacon, then place the top of the English muffin on top and press down. Repeat until all four sandwiches are assembled.

4. Tightly wrap with plastic wrap and then place all four sandwiches in a gallon-size freezer bag and label "Breakfast Sandwiches" and the date they were made (see note).

5. To warm the sandwiches: Remove from the freezer and remove the bag and plastic wrap. Wrap each sandwich in a piece of paper towel and microwave on HIGH for 2 minutes. Allow to sit in the microwave for 1 minute, then remove and enjoy.

SPICY BREAKFAST HASH

Potatoes
Chorizo Sausage
Vegetable Oil
Jalapeño
Eggs

SERVES 4

Jump-start your day with this flavorful Southwest-inspired hash. While in college, I made breakfast hash on the weekends for my best friend and me, but it was years later that my husband perfected this recipe. He makes the best breakfast hash around. It is all about those crispy potatoes and the perfect blend of flavors. Even though this dish is a little more labor intensive, it is well worth the extra few minutes for a wonderful weekend breakfast.

2 large russet potatoes, skin on
2 chorizo sausage links (6 to 8 ounces)
3 tablespoons vegetable oil, divided
½ teaspoon salt
Pinch of freshly ground black pepper
1 jalapeño pepper, seeded and finely minced (see note)
4 large eggs

NOTES

I'd say the spice level of this dish is medium, so if you like it really spicy, add two jalapeños and leave some seeds in for extra spicy. I like my eggs over hard, or "ruined" as my husband likes to joke—I like when they're flipped and the yolk is popped. For the runny yolk and sunny-side up egg, I would suggest 4 to 5 minutes in the skillet.

1. Wash the potatoes and pat dry with a paper towel. Place the potatoes in a bowl or on a shallow plate and microwave, uncovered, on HIGH for 3 minutes. Flip the potatoes and microwave for an additional minute. Allow them to cool until you can touch them (I let them sit on the counter while browning the meat).

2. When you can touch the potatoes, cut them (leaving the skin on is okay) into ½- to 1-inch cubes (the smaller the cubes, the faster they'll cook) and set them aside.

3. In a large skillet, brown the chorizo sausages, poking them with a fork and turning them every so often, until they have browned on all sides, about 6 minutes. Remove from the skillet and place them on a plate to rest.

4. Heat 2 tablespoons of the vegetable oil in the skillet for 30 seconds, then add the potatoes in a single layer and sprinkle with salt and black pepper. Cook for 15 to 20 minutes, flipping only every so often so that the potato cubes form nice browned edges. Slice the chorizo into small pieces.

5. Add the remaining tablespoon of vegetable oil, the chorizo pieces, and the minced jalapeño. Cook for 5 minutes, then transfer the contents of the skillet to a bowl and set aside.

6. Crack the eggs into the skillet and cook to your desired level of doneness (see note).

7. Divide the hash among four plates. Top each with an egg and enjoy.

OVEN TOAD-IN-THE-HOLE PIZZAS

SERVES 4

There are many different names for toad in the hole, which is an egg inside a cut-out piece of bread. I've also heard it called bird in a nest, eggs on a raft, or sunshine toast. Whatever name you want to give these little oven pizzas, they make for one yummy breakfast. They're like healthier grilled cheese, but for breakfast.

4 slices whole-wheat bread
4 large eggs
3 slices provolone cheese
½ Roma tomato, sliced into
   4 slices (see note)
1 teaspoon Italian seasoning,
   store-bought or homemade
   (page 216)
½ teaspoon salt

NOTE

If you don't have a tomato, you could use a dollop of marinara sauce (store-bought or homemade; see page 219) on the little circles of bread.

1. Preheat the oven to 400°F. Line a baking sheet with a silicone baking mat or parchment paper.

2. Place the bread slices on the prepared baking sheet. Press a small glass or biscuit cutter into the center of a bread slice, run a knife around it, then remove the circle and place it next to the slice of bread on the baking sheet. Repeat until all the slices of bread have an empty hole in the middle.

3. Crack each egg into a hole.

4. Break or cut a slice of cheese into four to six pieces, then place the pieces around the edges of each egg-filled bread slice, reserving a little piece of cheese to place on a cut-out circle of bread. Place a tomato slice on each cut-out circle of bread. Repeat for the remaining bread.

5. Season the egg-filled pieces of bread and circles with the Italian seasoning and salt.

6. Bake for 15 to 20 minutes, or until the cheese is melted. Remove from the oven and allow to cool for a few minutes and serve.

SUN-DRIED TOMATO BREAKFAST PIZZA

Pizza Crust
Fire-Roasted Tomatoes
Mozzarella Cheese
Eggs
Sun-Dried Tomatoes

MAKES 1 PIZZA; SERVES 4

Pizza for breakfast? Yes, please! Breakfast pizza is one of my most loved dishes to make on the weekends for brunch. The cheese melts around the eggs and the flavors of the fire-roasted tomatoes and sun-dried tomatoes are phenomenal.

1 premade thin pizza crust
1 (14.5-ounce) can fire-roasted diced tomatoes, drained
2 cups shredded low-moisture, part-skim mozzarella cheese
4 large eggs
Pinch each of salt and freshly ground black pepper
1 handful sun-dried tomatoes, chopped (about 6 tomatoes; see note)

NOTE

Sometimes I put the sun-dried tomatoes over or under the cheese—it just depends on how you like them baked. I like when they turn dark and get a little crispy, so I put them on the top of the cheese. Under the cheese, they are still delicious but are a little softer. If you don't have any sun-dried tomatoes, you can still make this pizza and leave them off; this pizza is still a must-make and tastes great.

1. Preheat the oven to 450°F.
2. Lay the pizza crust on a baking sheet.
3. Spoon the fire-roasted tomatoes onto the pizza crust and sprinkle with the shredded cheese.
4. Make four little wells on the pizza, pushing aside the cheese and tomatoes, and crack the eggs into the wells. Pinch a little salt and pepper over the eggs.
5. Bake for 15 minutes, remove from the oven, and sprinkle the sun-dried tomato pieces over the pizza. Return the pizza to the oven and bake for another 5 minutes. Then remove from the oven, slice, and enjoy.

Honey
Coconut Oil
Oats
Trail Mix
Flaxseeds

TRAIL MIX GRANOLA

MAKES 2¼ CUPS GRANOLA; SERVES 3 TO 4

Homemade granola is delicious as a breakfast served with milk or on top of yogurt. The beauty of this granola is that it uses trail mix, so it is packed full of delicious flavors, such as peanuts and chocolate.

¼ cup honey
2 tablespoons coconut oil or
  vegetable oil
1 cup quick-cooking oats
1 cup trail mix (see note)
1 tablespoon flaxseeds
  (optional)

NOTE

I like to use a "little bit of every-thing" trail mix. Any trail mix will work—but I usually like one that includes some mixture of chocolate and dried fruit.

1. Preheat the oven to 325°F and line a baking sheet with parchment paper or a silicone baking mat.

2. In a small saucepan, melt the honey and coconut oil over medium heat until combined and easy to stir.

3. In a large bowl, combine the oats, trail mix, and flaxseeds. Pour the honey mixture over the dry mixture and stir to coat.

4. Spoon the mixture onto the prepared baking sheet, press flat, and bake for 10 minutes, then remove from the oven, stir, and bake for another 10 minutes. Remove from the oven and allow to cool completely before serving. Serve fresh or store in an airtight container.

YOGURT GRANOLA PARFAIT CUPS

Yogurt
Granola
Berries
Honey

SERVES 2

Parfait cups are so fancy; they always remind me of oceanside resorts and palm trees (not that I've had the chance to enjoy them in such locales; one can daydream, right?). However, one never sees a sloppily thrown-together parfait. How do they get the layers just so? Well, I'm going to share with you the trick for creating enviable layers and the recipe for my favorite yogurt granola parfait cups.

2½ cups vanilla yogurt, divided (see note)
1 cup granola, divided
1 cup berries, divided
2 teaspoons honey, divided

NOTES

I like using vanilla yogurt in this recipe, but any plain or flavored yogurt would work. To get the beautiful layers of yogurt, spoon the yogurt into a resealable plastic bag and then cut a bottom corner off the bag (yay—you've just made a piping bag), and then squeeze the yogurt into the glass.

1. Pipe about ½ cup yogurt into the bottom of a glass (see note), sprinkle in ¼ cup of the granola and then ¼ cup of the berries, and finally, pipe in another ¼ cup of yogurt. Repeat to prepare a second glass of parfait.

2. Drizzle 1 teaspoon of the honey onto each glass, on top of the yogurt, then top each glass with ¼ cup of the remaining granola and then ¼ cup of the remaining berries. Serve.

SALADS, STARTERS, AND SIDES

BROCCOLI APRICOT PECAN SALAD

Broccoli
Olive Oil
Garlic Salt
Dried Apricots
Pecan Halves

SERVES 4

When I ordered a roasted broccoli dish at a local farm-to-table restaurant, I never would have expected it to come out with dried apricots and nuts on it. But it did, and I was hooked. This salad is the perfect combination of savory with a hint of sweet, and it is oh so good.

1 head broccoli, cut into florets
2 tablespoons extra-virgin olive oil
¼ teaspoon salt
¼ teaspoon garlic salt
6 dried apricots, sliced
10 pecan halves, chopped

NOTE
This salad can be served warm or cold.

1. Preheat the oven to 425°F. Line a baking sheet with aluminum foil.

2. Place the broccoli florets on the baking sheet, drizzle the olive oil over them, and sprinkle with the salt and garlic salt. Bake for 15 minutes.

3. Remove from the oven and add the apricots and pecan halves to the baking sheet, then bake for an additional 5 minutes. Remove from the oven and serve.

Couscous
Chicken
Olive Oil
Avocado
Lemon

CHICKEN COUSCOUS AVOCADO SALAD

SERVES 4 TO 6

You know those deli counters at grocery stores that have a bunch of salads for sale? I used to love those. While I was growing up, when my mom would be at work late, my dad would pick up a bunch of different salads for us to have for dinner. This simple salad was one that always stuck with me: pearl couscous with chicken and avocados, finished with a drizzle of lemon juice that adds a little zip. It's so good and such an easy salad to make at home.

1 (4.7-ounce) box pearled or regular couscous mix with roasted garlic and olive oil
1 pound chicken tenders or breast, cubed
1 tablespoon extra-virgin olive oil
½ teaspoon salt
Pinch of freshly ground black pepper
1 avocado, peeled, pitted, and cubed
Juice of 1 lemon (see note)

1. Start by cooking the couscous mix according to the package instructions.

2. Meanwhile, in a medium skillet over high heat, heat the olive oil for 1 minute, then add the chicken cubes, salt, and pepper and cook, stirring occasionally, for 10 minutes, or until no more pink is visible and the chicken is cooked through.

3. When the couscous is done cooking, combine the couscous and chicken in a large bowl, add the avocado, drizzle with the lemon juice, stir, and then serve.

NOTES
This salad is great served warm or cold (it's great for lunches). I like it with a distinct lemon flavor; if you don't like a bold lemon flavor, start by adding only ½ lemon's worth of juice.

CREAMY POTATO AND KALE SALAD

SERVES 4

In this salad, mayonnaise is used instead of oil to roast the potatoes. It forms this beautiful crunchy crust on the potatoes. The complementing garlic and lemon flavors give this salad a real zippy flavor; it makes for one delicious side dish.

---

1 pound baby potatoes, cut in half
¼ cup mayonnaise (I use light mayonnaise)
2 teaspoons salt
¼ teaspoon freshly ground black pepper
4 garlic cloves, pressed
Zest of 1 lemon
2 cups kale, cut into 2-inch pieces

1. Preheat the oven to 400°F. Line a 9 x 13-inch baking dish with aluminum foil, spray with cooking spray, and set aside.

2. In a large bowl, combine the halved potatoes, mayonnaise, salt, pepper, garlic, and lemon zest. Stir so that all the potatoes are covered in mayo, then pour into the prepared baking dish and bake for 25 minutes.

3. Remove from the oven. With a spatula, flip or stir the potatoes, then bake for another 15 minutes.

4. Remove from the oven, add the kale, stir, and bake for 10 more minutes. Remove from the oven and serve.

CRISPY BACON AND BRUSSELS SPROUTS SALAD

SERVES 4

I don't know who started the rumor that Brussels sprouts weren't good, because it's simply not true. Brussels sprouts are incredibly delicious, and when made with crispy bacon and coated with this savory and slightly sweet sauce of Dijon mustard, maple syrup, and lemon juice, they're simply amazing. My husband says this salad is so good it's BS (get it . . . Brussels sprouts), ha-ha.

½ **pound bacon, chopped**
1 **pound Brussels sprouts, ends removed, halved (see note)**
1½ **tablespoons Dijon mustard**
1 **tablespoon pure maple syrup**
Juice of ½ lemon

NOTES
You want the Brussels sprouts to be roughly the same size, so if there are a few that are really small, don't halve them; alternatively, if there are some that are really big, halve or even quarter them.

1. In a large skillet over high heat, cook the bacon, stirring occasionally, for 5 minutes, or until it starts to turn brown. Add the Brussels sprouts and cook, stirring occasionally, for an additional 5 minutes.

2. In a small bowl, whisk together the mustard, maple syrup, and lemon juice. Pour over the Brussels sprouts mixture and cook for 5 minutes, then remove from the heat and serve.

GREEN BEAN AND TOASTED ALMOND SALAD

Almonds
Olive Oil
Green Beans
Garlic
Feta Cheese

SERVES 4

If there is one vegetable I truly love, it is green beans. They have a fantastic crunch to them and really combine well with a few simple ingredients to make one incredible side dish. This salad is one of my favorite sides: a little crunch from the green beans and almonds and a little tartness from the feta—deeeelish!

¼ cup naturally sliced almonds
2 tablespoons extra-virgin olive oil
1 pound fresh green beans, ends trimmed
2 garlic cloves, pressed
½ teaspoon salt
2 ounces feta cheese, crumbled

1. Preheat the oven to 350°F. Line a baking sheet with aluminum foil, spread the sliced almonds on the prepared baking sheet, and bake for 5 minutes, or until golden brown.

2. Heat the olive oil in a large skillet over medium-high heat, add the green beans, garlic, and salt, and cook, stirring occasionally, for 12 to 15 minutes, or until slightly soft and some of the green beans have browned. Remove from the heat, sprinkle the feta cheese and almonds over the green beans, and serve.

Salsa
Ground Turkey
Romaine Lettuce
Shredded Cheese
Tortilla Chips

TURKEY TACO SALAD

SERVES 4

My friend who is a busy mom taught me how to make this salad, and now I make it all the time on nights when I'm short on time but want a delicious salad. It takes a total of 20 minutes to make and is great for a quick dinner salad or for lunch the next day.

1 cup salsa, store-bought or homemade (page 220), divided
1 pound extra-lean ground turkey (see notes)
6 to 8 cups romaine or greens/lettuce of choice
1 cup shredded cheese (I use Mexican blend cheese, Cheddar, or pepper Jack)
2 cups tortilla chips

1. Pour ½ cup of the salsa into a large skillet. Add the ground turkey and cook on high heat, breaking it up as it cooks, for 15 minutes, or until the turkey is cooked through.

2. Place the lettuce in a large bowl or four small bowls.

3. When the turkey is done, spoon on top of the lettuce, pour the remaining ½ cup of salsa on top of the turkey, then add the cheese and tortilla chips (I like to crush some of the tortilla chips).

4. Mix the salad and enjoy.

NOTES

Instead of using ground turkey, you could make salsa slow cooker chicken as a topping: Simply put 1 pound of chicken breast in a slow cooker and cover it with ½ cup of the salsa and a pinch of salt. Cook on LOW for 8 hours or on HIGH for 4 hours, then shred when done. This salad is good served with either warm or cold cooked ground turkey. If making this salad for eating at a later time, just cook the ground turkey and salsa and store it in an airtight container in the fridge until ready to use. You could use a number of add-ins with this salad; for example, a dollop of sour cream or some olives—the possibilities are endless.

BROCCOLI CHEDDAR SOUP

Broccoli
Carrots
Chicken Stock
Heavy Cream
Sharp Cheddar Cheese

SERVES 4 TO 6

As soon as the weather starts getting colder I find myself craving soup. Warm and comforting soup like this broccoli cheddar soup immediately prepares me for the cold weather and snow that is sure to come. This soup is hearty enough that it can be served for dinner and would be great for dunking toast in.

1 (12-ounce) package steam-in-bag broccoli florets
1 cup frozen carrots
2½ cups fat-free, sodium-reduced chicken stock (see notes)
1 cup heavy cream
¼ teaspoon salt
2 cups shredded sharp cheddar cheese

NOTES
For vegetarians, make with vegetable stock instead of chicken stock. If you want a thicker soup, add ½ cup less stock.

1. Microwave the broccoli and carrots according to the package instructions and set aside.

2. In a large pot, bring the chicken stock, cream, and salt to a boil. Stir in the cheese and allow it to melt for 2 minutes while stirring, then stir in the broccoli and carrots and remove from the heat.

3. Carefully pour the contents of the pot into a food processor or blender and pulsate for 5 seconds, until no large pieces of broccoli remain. Pour back into the pot, ladle into soup bowls, and serve.

CHEDDAR BISCUIT CRACKERS

MAKES 24 CRACKERS

"These are so good, they taste exactly like crackers my grandmother used to make," exclaimed one of my girlfriends when I brought these to a party. Little cracker biscuits packed with cheddar flavor, they're reminiscent of after-school snacks. There's a little zip to them and they're truly irresistible.

1 cup all-purpose flour, plus more for rolling

1 cup shredded sharp cheddar cheese

1 tablespoon cornstarch

¼ teaspoon cayenne pepper

½ teaspoon salt

½ cup (1 stick; 4 ounces) unsalted butter, cold and cut into 8 pieces

3 tablespoons ice water

NOTES

Instead of freezing for 30 minutes and then slicing and baking the crackers, you can leave the plastic-wrapped dough in the refrigerator overnight and then slice and bake them the next day. Baking times may vary depending on how thickly you have cut your crackers. I like to make them thin (about ⅛ inch thick).

1. Preheat the oven to 350°F (see notes). Line two baking sheets with silicone baking mats or parchment paper and set aside.

2. In a food processor, combine the flour, cheese, cornstarch, cayenne, and salt and pulsate to combine, 5 seconds.

3. Add the pieces of butter and pulsate until a crumbly dough forms, 10 seconds, then with the motor running, slowly pour in the ice water and pulsate until a dough ball forms, 10 seconds. Carefully remove the dough from the food processor and form into two logs, each about 6 inches long, and cover with plastic wrap. Freeze for 30 minutes, then remove from the freezer and slice each log into thin crackers.

4. Lay the dough disks on the prepared baking sheets and bake for 15 minutes, or until the edges are starting to brown (see notes). Remove from the oven and allow to cool before serving.

CHEESY GARLIC BREAD

Italian Bread
Butter
Garlic Salt
Italian Blend
Shredded Cheese

MAKES 8 SLICES GARLIC BREAD
(EASILY SCALED UP OR DOWN)

Cheesy garlic bread—the perfect side to pastas and salads alike. If you're anything like me, I bet you love garlic bread but perhaps dislike when there's so much garlic that your mouth hurts. Fear that no more, my friend; I am going to share with you the secret for having deliciously garlicky bread without it being overpowering: garlic salt. That simple ingredient makes it the best garlic bread ever.

½ loaf Italian bread (8 large slices)
4 tablespoons unsalted butter
2 teaspoons garlic salt
1 cup Italian blend shredded cheese or shredded mozzarella

1. Preheat the oven to 400°F. Line a baking sheet with aluminum foil or a silicone baking mat and place the bread slices on it.

2. In a small, microwave-safe bowl, microwave the butter, 20 to 30 seconds, on HIGH, until melted, and add the garlic salt; stir to combine.

3. Spread the garlic butter on the bread slices (I just use a butter knife for this).

4. Sprinkle the cheese evenly over the garlic butter and bake for 10 minutes. Remove from the oven and allow to cool for a minute or two, then serve and enjoy.

Butter

Leeks

Cream Cheese

Sour Cream

Italian- or Mexican-
Blend Shredded
Cheese

CHEESY LEEK DIP

MAKES ABOUT 3 CUPS DIP; SERVES 12 TO 20

This dip is a party favorite. Whenever I have a family get-together or a party, I get asked whether I'm bringing that "cheesy leek dip." The answer is always yes, because this dip is amazing. It came about after having a cheesy leek spread at a restaurant and loving what the addition of leeks did for the dip—they added an incredible flavor. What's great about this recipe is that it can be made in either a mini slow cooker or the oven. Your guests will love this unique dip and will dip chip after chip into the cheesy goodness.

1 tablespoon unsalted butter

2 leeks, well cleaned and chopped

1 teaspoon salt

8 ounces regular or reduced-fat cream cheese

1 cup regular or reduced-fat sour cream

1 cup Italian- or Mexican-blend shredded cheese

NOTES

If you want to add a little heat to your dip, sprinkle in a little cayenne pepper.

1. In a medium skillet, melt the butter over high heat. Add the leeks, sprinkle with salt, and cook until soft and some leeks start to brown on the edges, about 5 minutes.

2. **Slow cooker method:** Place the cooked leeks, cream cheese, sour cream, and shredded cheese in the slow cooker and cook on HIGH for an hour, stirring every 20 minutes, then lower the heat to WARM and serve with pita chips or crackers.

3. **Oven method:** Preheat the oven to 350°F. In a large bowl, combine the cooked leeks, cream cheese, sour cream, and shredded cheese and stir. Spoon the dip into an 8-inch square baking dish and bake for 30 minutes, or until bubbly and starting to brown around the edges. Remove from the oven and serve with pita chips or crackers.

HEARTS OF PALM AND ARTICHOKE DIP

Cream Cheese
Sour Cream
Hearts of Palm
Artichoke Hearts
Italian-Blend
Shredded Cheese

MAKES ABOUT 3 CUPS DIP; SERVES 10 TO 15

Most people have heard of spinach and artichoke dip, but have you heard of hearts of palm and artichoke dip? I'm here to introduce you to an incredible dip that you'll want to share with all your friends and family. When my mom told me I had to try hearts of palm, I thought I had heard wrong, but she assured me I hadn't and that I should go to the grocery store and seek them out. Sure enough, she was right (thanks, Mom!).

8 ounces cream cheese, softened
½ cup sour cream
1 cup hearts of palm, chopped (see notes)
12 ounces marinated artichoke hearts, drained and chopped
1 cup Italian-blend shredded cheese, divided
½ teaspoon salt

NOTES

Hearts of palm are a vegetable harvested from the core of the palm tree. Soft and about an inch in diameter, they look like white rods. They are a great addition to dips, adding a smooth and creamy texture that complements the artichoke hearts perfectly. They may be found in most major grocery stores, either by the canned vegetables or in the Mediterranean or Hispanic sections. This dip can also be made with spinach instead of hearts of palm, substituted in an equal amount.

1. Preheat the oven to 400°F.

2. In a large bowl, stir together the cream cheese and sour cream, then stir in the hearts of palm, artichoke hearts, ½ cup of the shredded cheese, and the salt, until combined.

3. Spoon the dip into an 8-inch square baking dish and sprinkle the remaining ½ cup of shredded cheese on top.

4. Bake for 20 to 25 minutes, or until the edges and top start to turn golden brown. Remove from the oven and serve with a side of pita chips, tortilla chips, or crackers.

MEDITERRANEAN DIP

Feta Cheese
Tomato
Olive Oil
Scallions
Mediterranean-
Spiced Sea Salt

**MAKES ABOUT 2 CUPS DIP; SERVES 10 TO 15
(DOUBLES EASILY)**

My favorite recipe when I am short on time and need to bring something to a party or get-together is this Mediterranean dip. It comes together in a flash, is a no-bake dish, and is loved by all; it is truly an all-around amazing appetizer.

---

1 cup feta cheese, crumbled
1 large or 2 small beefsteak
   tomatoes, chopped
1½ tablespoons extra-virgin
   olive oil
3 scallions, chopped
1 teaspoon Mediterranean-
   spiced sea salt, store-
   bought (see notes) or
   homemade (page 216)

1. Sprinkle the cheese onto a plate with a lip or in a shallow bowl or serving dish. Top with the chopped tomato and drizzle with the olive oil.

2. Sprinkle with the scallions and then with the Mediterranean spiced sea salt. Serve with a spoon and pita chips, tortilla chips, or even as a bruschetta topping on bread.

NOTES
McCormick makes the blend of Mediterranean spiced sea salt that I use, but I've also used other blends—you want it to contain oregano and thyme, among other flavorings. This dip is also great if you want to make it ahead and let it sit in the refrigerator.

NACHOS

SERVES 8

Game day just wouldn't be the same without nachos. The best nachos are ones with crunchy chips and ooey-gooey cheese. The trick to achieving the perfect crunch is to prebake the chips and then bake them again to melt the cheese.

¾ (13-ounce) bag tortilla chips
1 (16-ounce) can refried beans
2 cups Mexican-blend
   shredded cheese
½ cup sour cream (see note)
½ cup salsa, store-bought or
   homemade (page 220)

NOTE

If you want to drizzle on the sour cream like a thick sauce, mix the sour cream with 2 tablespoons of water in a bowl. Spoon the mixture into a small, resealable plastic bag. Cut one bottom corner off the bag (yay—you've just made a piping bag!) and squeeze the sour cream over the nachos.

1. Preheat the oven to 350°F. Line a baking sheet with aluminum foil.

2. Spread the tortilla chips evenly on the prepared baking sheet and spoon dollops of refried beans over the chips.

3. Bake for 10 minutes. Remove from the oven and sprinkle the cheese over the chips and beans. Bake for 5 to 10 minutes, or until the cheese has melted.

4. Remove from the oven and dollop with the sour cream and salsa.

POLENTA PIZZA BITES

Polenta
Italian Seasoning
Shredded Mozzarella Cheese
Tomato

MAKES 24 TO 30 POLENTA PIZZA BITES

Whenever I need to bring a fancy appetizer that's not a dip and I'm really short on time, this is what I bring. It's totally adorable, not to mention delicious, and incredibly easy to make. You simply slice, assemble, and bake, and voilà, you have yourself an appetizer or starter dish that looks as if you spent hours making it (while in reality it only took you mere minutes to prepare).

1 (18-ounce) tube precooked polenta (see notes)
1 tablespoon Italian seasoning, store-bought or homemade (page 216)
1 cup shredded low-moisture, part-skim mozzarella cheese
1 large tomato

NOTES

Precooked polenta can be found next to the pasta or in the Italian section of most grocery stores. Alternatively, you can put the tomato slices on before the cheese. These polenta pizza bites can also be made ahead of time and then microwaved to reheat before your party.

1. Preheat the oven to 400°F. Line a baking sheet with aluminum foil and spray with cooking spray.

2. Slice the polenta into thin slices and place on the prepared baking sheet. Sprinkle with the Italian seasoning.

3. Sprinkle the cheese over the polenta (I measure out the cheese and then pinch a little on top of each polenta slice; see notes).

4. Slice the tomato into thin slices and then cut each slice in half. Place ½ slice on each cheese-covered polenta slice.

5. Bake for 15 minutes, then remove from the oven and allow to sit for 2 minutes. Carefully transfer to a plate and serve.

PEPPERONI PIZZA POCKETS

MAKES 18 TO 24 PIZZA POCKETS

I've always loved snack time, and these pepperoni pizza pockets make for an awesome snack; kids and adults alike go crazy for them because they're mini pizzas wrapped in a flaky crust, and who doesn't love pizza? These are also fantastic for a game day snack.

2 (2-crust) packages premade, prerolled piecrust (a total of 4 crusts)
1½ cups pizza sauce, divided
1 cup sliced pepperoni (45 to 55 pieces; see note)
1 cup shredded mozzarella cheese
1 large egg yolk
1 tablespoon water

NOTE
For a vegetarian version, simply skip the pepperoni and add more cheese for the filling.

1. Preheat the oven to 350°F. Line a baking sheet with a silicone baking mat or parchment paper and set aside.

2. Start by unrolling one piecrust onto a cutting board. Cut out circles, using a biscuit cutter or tracing around the rim of a glass (I get eight to ten circles per piecrust).

3. Spread a spoonful of pizza sauce on a circle of pie dough, then place two or three pieces of pepperoni on top of the sauce and a heaping pinch of cheese on top of the pepperoni. Take another dough circle, place it on top of the cheese, and pinch the edges closed (you don't want the filling oozing out when baking, so make sure there are no gaps).

4. Place the sealed pocket on the prepared baking sheet and, using a sharp knife, cut a little slit on the top.

5. Repeat the process to form all the pizza pockets, placing them about an inch apart on the baking sheet.

6. In a small bowl, whisk together the egg yolk and water to form an egg wash. Brush the egg wash on top of all the pizza pockets.

7. Bake for 20 to 25 minutes, or until the tops of the pizza pockets are golden brown. Allow to cool for a few minutes, then serve with the remaining pizza sauce for dipping.

MASHED POTATOES

Potatoes
Parsnip
Butter
Milk
Sour Cream

SERVES 4

There's something to be said about creamy, perfectly mashed homemade potatoes. What's to be said is that you will be loved by all. Mashed potatoes are a quintessential side dish and are perfected with this recipe because of its secret ingredient: a parsnip. Parsnip is a root vegetable closely related to the carrot (in fact, it looks like a white carrot and can be found next to the carrots in most major grocery stores) and gives mashed potatoes that extra flavor flair; it's subtle but definitely makes the BEST mashed potatoes.

2 pounds russet or yellow
  potatoes (3 to 4 medium
  potatoes), peeled, cut, and
  quartered (see notes)
1 parsnip, peeled, cut, and
  quartered
3 tablespoons unsalted butter
¼ cup milk
¼ cup sour cream
1 teaspoon salt

1. Bring a large pot of water to a boil over high heat. Add the potatoes and parsnip pieces, and bring back to a boil. Boil for 15 minutes, or until the potatoes are tender when poked with a fork (the fork should go in easily).

2. Drain the water and return the vegetables to the pot.

3. Add the butter and let it melt for a minute, then add the milk, sour cream, and salt. With a hand mixer or potato masher, mix until smooth and creamy, about 1 minute (see notes), then serve.

NOTES

The smaller you cut the potatoes, the faster they cook. I usually cut each potato into quarters or sixths. I prefer to use a hand mixer to mash the potatoes; I've found it really helps with the consistency and making them silky smooth. Sometimes there may be a little piece or strand of parsnip that doesn't mash into the mixture; simply remove it.

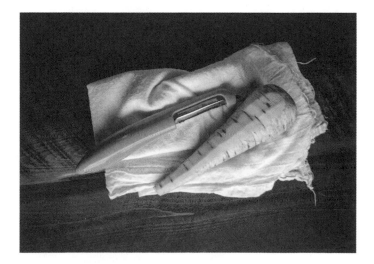

LOADED TATER TOTS

Tater Tots
Bacon
Mexican-Blend Cheese
Sour Cream
Salsa

SERVES 8 TO 10

It's game day and you have guests coming over. What to make? These loaded Tater Tots. Little taters are baked with bacon and then covered in ooey-gooey cheese and are served with a side of sour cream and salsa. They only take a few minutes to prepare, allowing you to enjoy the game with your guests.

---

1 (32-ounce) package Tater Tots or similar product
½ pound bacon, cut into small pieces (see note)
2 cups Mexican-blend shredded cheese or shredded sharp Cheddar cheese
1 cup sour cream
1 cup salsa, store-bought or homemade (page 220)

1. Preheat the oven to 400°F. Line a baking sheet with aluminum foil. Spray with cooking spray.

2. Spread out the Tater Tots on the baking sheet and sprinkle the bacon pieces on top of them.

3. Bake for 25 minutes, then loosen and flip the Tater Tots and bacon and sprinkle with the cheese. Bake for 5 more minutes, or until the cheese has melted.

4. Remove from the oven and serve with sour cream and salsa in bowls on the side.

NOTE
I use kitchen scissors to cut the bacon.

POTATO WEDGES & CHEESY SAUCE

**Russet Potatoes
Vegetable Oil
Garlic Salt
Paprika
Velveeta Cheese**

SERVES 6 TO 8

Cheesy fries—probably one of the best sides ever. Who doesn't love a crispy potato wedge that is dipped in cheesy goodness? Definitely not any of my friends, I can tell you that much. This is the perfect side to burgers (such as the BBQ Apple Cheddar Sliders, page 91).

4 russet potatoes
1 to 2 tablespoons
   vegetable oil
1 teaspoon salt
½ teaspoon garlic salt
½ teaspoon paprika (see
   notes)
8 slices Velveeta cheese

NOTES

If you like a little heat in your potato wedges, use chipotle chile powder instead of paprika. Leaving the skin on the potatoes, I cut each potato lengthwise into quarters, and then each quarter into two or three wedges, which yields 10 to 12 wedges per potato.

1. Preheat the oven to 400°F. Line a baking sheet with aluminum foil and place a wire cooling rack on top of the aluminum foil.

2. Slice the potatoes into wedges (see notes), rinse, pat them dry with a paper towel, and place them in a large bowl.

3. Pour in the vegetable oil and stir so that the potatoes are coated with oil, then sprinkle with the salt, garlic salt, and paprika. Stir so that the wedges are evenly coated with the seasonings.

4. Transfer the potatoes from the bowl to the rack-topped baking sheet and arrange them in a single layer.

5. Bake for 15 minutes, then remove from the oven and flip the wedges with tongs or a fork. Bake for an additional 10 minutes, or until browned edges are visible.

6. Remove from the oven and make the cheese sauce while the potato wedges are cooling a little (do not make the sauce ahead of time or the cheese will harden as it cools): Unwrap the cheese slices and put into a medium, microwave-safe bowl (glass bowls work really well). Cover tightly with plastic wrap and microwave for 2½ minutes on HIGH. Carefully lift one side of the plastic wrap (steam will escape as you lift it, so be careful not to burn yourself—I wear oven mitts and use a fork to lift the wrap) to see whether all the cheese has melted. If all the cheese is melted, carefully remove the plastic wrap all together, stir, and serve. If not all the cheese is melted, re-cover it with its plastic wrap and microwave for an additional 15 seconds, then check again, stir, and serve on the side of the potatoes.

ROSEMARY GARLIC PARMESAN FRITES

SERVES 4

When I hear the word *frites*, I immediately conjure up images of fancy French bistros where one gets skinny fries as a side. And immediately after thinking of frites I want some, these frites in particular. They've got a great crunch and are a fantastic side.

---

4 tablespoons extra-virgin
   olive oil, divided
4 medium to large russet or
   Idaho potatoes
2 garlic cloves, pressed
¼ cup Parmesan cheese,
   grated
1 teaspoon salt
1 tablespoon fresh rosemary
   (from about 2 big sprigs)

NOTE
*These are great for dipping in
some homemade Quick Ketchup
(page 217).*

---

1. Preheat the oven to 450°F. Line a baking sheet with aluminum foil and spread 1 tablespoon of the olive oil over the foil.

2. Slice the potatoes very thinly into matchsticks and place in a large bowl.

3. Add the remaining 3 tablespoons of olive oil, garlic, cheese, salt, and rosemary to the potatoes and stir until all the potatoes are coated with the olive oil and seasonings.

4. Pour onto the prepared baking sheet and bake for 15 minutes, then remove from the oven, flip the frites, and bake for another 15 minutes. Remove from the oven, transfer to a serving plate, and enjoy.

SWEET POTATO FRIES

Sweet Potatoes
Olive Oil
Chili Powder
Paprika
Cinnamon

SERVES 4

Sweet potato fries make a fantastic side, with a great smoky flavor and hint of sweetness; they go great with burgers or chicken. Even if you thought you didn't like sweet potatoes, try them in these baked fries and your opinion will be changed.

2 large sweet potatoes (about 2½ pounds)
3 tablespoons extra-virgin olive oil
1 teaspoon chili powder
1 teaspoon paprika
½ teaspoon ground cinnamon
¼ teaspoon salt

NOTE

I cut each sweet potato lengthwise into quarters, and then each quarter into two or three wedges, which yields 10 to 12 wedges per sweet potato.

1. Preheat the oven to 425°F. Line a baking sheet with aluminum foil and set aside.

2. Peel and cut the sweet potatoes into wedges (see note) and put into a large bowl.

3. Drizzle the olive oil onto the sweet potatoes and stir, then sprinkle with the chili powder, paprika, cinnamon, and salt and stir so that all the sweet potatoes are evenly coated with the seasonings.

4. Transfer to the prepared baking sheet, arranging all the sweet potatoes in one layer. Bake for 10 minutes, then flip the sweet potatoes and bake for another 10 to 15 minutes, or until tender when poked with a fork. Remove from the oven and serve.

BROCCOLI DIVINE

SERVES 10 TO 12 AS A SIDE

For our holidays, the menu may always change slightly, but this one truly comforting dish—broccoli topped with Cheddar and crispy buttery crumbles, and then baked to perfection—is always a staple. While I was growing up, my mother taught my three sisters and me how to make it. Now, no matter where we spend our holidays (with our new in-laws or at family gatherings), whenever we send one another pictures of the spread, you can always spot this dish in the background. Our holidays would just not be complete without it.

2 (16-ounce) bags frozen broccoli florets, thawed
1 (10¾-ounce) can condensed cheddar cheese soup
4 tablespoons unsalted butter
½ cup Italian seasoned or plain bread crumbs
1 cup shredded sharp cheddar cheese

1. Preheat the oven to 400°F. Line a baking sheet with aluminum foil and place the thawed broccoli florets on the sheet in three rows (or you could just scatter it onto the sheet).

2. Spoon the condensed soup directly from the can over the broccoli.

3. In a small saucepan over high heat, melt the butter, 3 minutes. Turn off the heat, add the bread crumbs, and stir until combined. Spoon the bread crumb mixture over the broccoli, then sprinkle the cheese on top.

4. Bake the broccoli for 20 minutes. Remove from the oven, serve, and enjoy.

STOVETOP MAC AND CHEESE

Elbow Macaroni
Butter
Flour
Milk
Sharp Cheddar Cheese

SERVES 6 TO 8 AS A SIDE

There are probably not enough pages in this book for me to profess my love for this recipe. It is everything you want in a mac and cheese—it's super creamy and comforting, and it is so easy to make. It's a one-pot stovetop recipe and is loved by all (even those picky eaters!). This dish goes great as a side to "Unfried" Cornflake Chicken (page 122) or can be served by itself, because, hello, it is mac and cheese—need I say more?

---

1 pound elbow macaroni
3 tablespoons unsalted butter
¼ cup all-purpose flour
1 teaspoon salt
1½ cups milk, plus more if needed
2 cups shredded sharp cheddar cheese (see note)

NOTE

I typically buy white cheddar for this recipe, but any sharp cheddar will work. If you use orange cheddar, the mac and cheese will be more orangey in color than pictured.

---

1. In a large pot, cook the pasta according to the package instructions, drain, and leave in the colander.

2. In the now empty large pot, melt the butter over medium-high heat, about 1 minute. When the butter is almost all melted, add the flour and salt. Whisk until it reaches a paste-like consistency, then slowly pour in the milk, still whisking, and let it come together, bringing to a slow boil, 4 to 5 minutes.

3. As soon as the milk starts to boil, add the cheese and stir a few times. If the mixture is too thick (it should be thick enough to coat a spoon, but thin enough to drip from the spoon), add another ¼ to ½ cup of milk, then add the pasta back to the pot and stir so that the macaroni is coated with the cheese sauce. Remove from the heat and let cool for a few minutes, then serve and enjoy.

CHEESY BACON POTATOES

SERVES 8 TO 10

Have you ever had a loaded baked potato? They're pretty great, but they take forever to make. These cheesy bacon potatoes are exactly like a loaded baked potato but in casserole form and take only 35 minutes to bake. Whenever we host a football-viewing party, these are on the menu; they are cheesy bacony potato goodness.

4 to 5 russet potatoes
1 teaspoon salt
½ pound applewood-smoked
    bacon, chopped
2 cups Mexican-blend
    shredded cheese
1 cup sour cream, for topping
1 bunch scallions, finely
    chopped, for topping

NOTE

The smaller you cube the potatoes, the faster they bake. I have found that the best size cubes are about 1 inch, or about 12 cubes per potato. I leave the skin on; it cuts back on prep time.

1. Preheat the oven to 425°F.

2. Cube the potatoes (see note) and place in a 9 x 13-inch baking dish. Sprinkle the salt over the potatoes and add the chopped bacon. Bake for 15 minutes, then remove from the oven, stir, and return to the oven to bake for an additional 15 minutes.

3. Remove from the oven, sprinkle the cheese over the potatoes and bacon, and bake for 5 minutes, or until the cheese has melted.

4. Remove from the oven and allow to cool for a few minutes before serving. Serve with a side of sour cream and scallions.

TOMATO AND SWEET POTATO TIAN

Garlic Olive Oil
Tomatoes
Sweet Potatoes
Italian Seasoning
Italian-Blend
Shredded Cheese

SERVES 6 TO 8 AS A SIDE

Traditionally featuring thinly sliced vegetables layered with herbs and cheese and then baked, *tian* is a French word that describes both a shallow casserole dish as well as the food it contains. I love making this vegetarian side dish with tomato and sweet potato slices; it goes really well as a side dish and can be made with either sweet potatoes or regular potatoes.

---

1 tablespoon garlic-flavored olive oil or just plain extra-virgin olive oil

3 Roma tomatoes, thinly sliced

2 large sweet potatoes, peeled and thinly sliced

1 tablespoon Italian seasoning, store-bought or homemade (page 216)

½ teaspoon salt

1 cup Italian-blend shredded cheese

1. Preheat the oven to 375°F. Coat an 11-inch oval baking dish with the olive oil.

2. Around the outside edge of the baking dish, start arranging the vegetable slices, standing them up. I place them as follows: one tomato slice, then two sweet potato slices, then repeat, until the baking dish has all the vegetables in it. Alternatively, you can layer the slices flat on top of one another.

3. Sprinkle the Italian seasoning and salt over the vegetables and then sprinkle with the cheese. Bake for 45 minutes or until the cheese has melted and has started to brown around the edges (poke vegetables with a fork to make sure the vegetables are soft). Remove from the oven and serve.

MAINS
AND
MEATS

BBQ APPLE CHEDDAR SLIDERS

Ground Beef
BBQ Sauce
Buns
Apple
Cheddar Cheese

MAKES 8 SLIDERS OR 4 REGULAR-SIZE BURGERS

Burgers are such a family favorite meal and these sliders are no exception. They have a delicious flavor combination of the BBQ burgers and crunchy apple slices and can be made into mini sliders or regular burgers. Next time you're in need of a fun family dinner recipe, look no further than these sliders.

1 pound lean ground beef
¼ cup BBQ sauce
8 slider buns or 4 hamburger
  buns
1 apple, thinly sliced
2 slices cheddar cheese,
  quartered

NOTE
These sliders pair very well with a side of Potato Wedges & Cheesy Sauce (page 75) or Sweet Potato Fries (page 79).

1. In a bowl, mix together the ground beef and BBQ sauce, then form into 8 small patties or 4 regular-size patties.

2. In a nonstick pan over high heat, fry the patties for 5 minutes, then flip and cook for another 5 minutes.

3. Toast the buns, if you wish, and slice the apple into very thin strips, discarding the core.

4. To assemble, place some apple slices on each bottom bun, place a burger on top of the apple, add a slice of cheese and the top bun, and enjoy.

BEEF DIP SANDWICHES

MAKES 4 SANDWICHES (SEE NOTES)

There's something special about dipping a big sandwich into a tasty broth. It's hearty and makes for a delicious dinner. I love these sandwiches because I simply put ingredients into a slow cooker and set it on LOW before work and then come home to a fall-apart beef in delectable broth. It takes less than five minutes to assemble the sandwiches and voilà, dinner is served.

1 (2- to 3-pound) beef rump
   roast
1 (32-ounce) container beef
   stock
1 (1-ounce) packet dried
   French onion soup mix
4 hoagie rolls
4 slices provolone cheese

NOTES

This recipe is easily scaled up to serve more or make additional meat for sandwiches. The amount of broth is enough for up to eight sandwiches, so you could use up to a 6-pound roast and then just get more rolls and slices of cheese. If you like sliced beef instead of shredded beef, I would suggest cooking the beef on HIGH for 5 hours instead of on LOW for 8 hours; then you will be able to slice it.

1. Put the beef rump roast in a slow cooker and pour in the beef stock and onion soup mix, stirring until no chunks of soup mix remain. Set the slow cooker to LOW and cook for 8 hours (see notes).

2. To set up the sandwiches when the beef is done, cut the rolls in half and place one slice of cheese on each bottom bun. Set out little bowls on each plate and ladle one or two ladlefuls of the broth mixture from the slow cooker into the bowls.

3. Carefully remove the roast from the slow cooker and slice on a cutting board. Place the meat on top of the cheese and cover with the top roll, then serve with a dipping bowl and enjoy.

POT ROAST WITH VEGETABLES

SERVES 4 TO 6

Gathering around the table for Sunday family dinners was always a tradition we had in my house-hold that I loved while growing up. I'm lucky enough to have in-laws who to this day also do family dinners. My in-laws live a whopping five minutes away from us, and every Sunday, the entire family gets together to share a meal. To me, a good family dinner is one that everyone enjoys. The beauty of a pot roast dinner is that it is super easy to make: The hands-on prep time is minimal and then the roast cooks to perfection with no additional attention required. Gather your family around and make this comforting classic recipe that everyone is sure to love.

1 (3- to 5-pound) beef chuck roast

1 tablespoon plus about ½ teaspoon salt, divided

2 to 3 tablespoons extra-virgin olive oil, plus more for the vegetables

6 to 8 whole carrots, ends removed and cut into chunks

1½ pounds baby or fingerling potatoes, left whole and unpeeled (see notes)

3 cups beef stock

Freshly ground black pepper

1. Start by getting the roast ready to cook: Remove the silver skin first and then pat 1 tablespoon of salt on the roast; if your entire roast isn't covered, add a little more salt (see notes).

2. Next, spoon the olive oil over the salted roast and pat into it so that the whole roast is covered in olive oil (see notes).

3. Place the oiled and salted roast in a Dutch oven and sear over high heat until browned on all sides, about 5 minutes. To brown the meat, simply let it sit for a few minutes on each side; don't constantly flip it. Use only tongs to flip the roast, don't poke it with a fork, which will cause the meat juices to escape.

4. Transfer the browned roast to a plate. In the now-empty Dutch oven, add a dash of oil, the carrots and potatoes, and about ½ teaspoon of salt. Cook until the vegetables start to brown a little, about 5 minutes.

NOTES

If using bigger potatoes, cut them into halves or fourths so that they're uniformly sized chunks. To remove the silver skin on the roast, start at one end of the roast: Make a little prick into the silver skin and then pick it up in a pinching motion and cut underneath it to remove it, slowly pushing the blade of your knife away from you toward the other end of the meat. Presalting the meat brings out the flavors while it cooks. Never prepepper your pot roast; pepper burns in the pan while browning, so postpone peppering until after you have browned the meat. Oiling the meat, not the pot, will help make that amazing crust when browning the pot roast. Browning your roast before adding the other ingredients creates that amazing roasted meat crust and flavor on the outside, with juicy meat on the inside.

5. Gently push the vegetables to the sides of the Dutch oven and nestle the roast in the middle, pour the beef stock over the meat and vegetables so that they are about half to three-quarters covered with liquid. Sprinkle with pepper.

6. Cook, covered, on medium-low heat for 4 hours, or until the meat falls apart when touched with a fork.

7. Alternatively, you could make this dish in a slow cooker. To do so, brown the meat and cook the vegetables a little, and then put the roast and vegetables into a slow cooker and cook on LOW for 6 to 7 hours, until the meat falls apart when poked with a fork.

8. To serve, remove a few vegetables from the pot and cut the desired amount of meat. Serve and enjoy.

BEEF STROGANOFF

Egg Noodles
Olive Oil
Top Sirloin Steak
Beef Stock
Sour Cream

SERVES 4

From start to finish, this comfortingly delicious dish takes less than 30 minutes to make, and on busy weeknights I'm all about quick meals like this. Plus it's super easy to make. You brown the beef, let it cook as you make the sauce in the same pan, and 20 minutes later, voilà, you have beef stroganoff, served over egg noodles (see notes).

½ **pound egg noodles**
1 **tablespoon extra-virgin olive oil**
1 **pound top sirloin steak, cut into strips**
1 **teaspoon salt**
¼ **teaspoon freshly ground black pepper**
1¾ **cups beef stock**
½ **cup sour cream**

NOTES

I serve this dish over egg noodles but it is also good served over rice or any pasta you have on hand. This dish is great served with a little sprinkling of Parmesan cheese over it.

1. Bring a pot of water to a boil and cook the egg noodles according to the package instructions.

2. In a large skillet (big enough to hold beef and stock), heat the olive oil over high heat for 2 minutes, then add the beef strips and sprinkle with salt and pepper. Stirring occasionally, cook the beef until it browns, about 5 minutes.

3. Move the beef to one side of the pan, and add the stock and the sour cream to the other side of the pan. With a whisk, combine the stock and sour cream in the pan so that no clumps remain. Evenly distribute the beef throughout the pan and continue to cook, stirring occasionally, for 10 to 15 minutes, or until the sauce boils around the edges and thickens.

4. To serve, divide the noodles among four bowls or onto plates with a lip (to catch the delicious sauce) and top with the beef and sauce (see notes).

RED WINE STEAK AND MUSHROOMS

SERVES 2

The very first Valentine's Day my husband and I spent together, we decided to stay in and beat the crowds at the restaurants and he said he was going to cook dinner. He made red wine steak and mushrooms and I was absolutely blown away by how delicious it was. It was so good that now on special occasions, this is always the dish I request. It's absolutely perfect for a special date night in.

2 rib-eye steaks (1½ to
   2 pounds total)
1½ teaspoons salt
¼ teaspoon freshly ground
   black pepper
1 tablespoon vegetable oil
2 tablespoons unsalted butter,
   divided (see notes)
¾ cup red wine or beef stock
8 ounces white mushrooms,
   sliced

NOTES

You can use less butter if you'd like. For steaks cooked to medium doneness, remove from the skillet when they reach 155°F on a meat thermometer.

1. Pat the steaks dry with a paper towel, leave on or trim off the fat, and sprinkle both sides of the steaks with salt and pepper. Let rest for 10 to 30 minutes before cooking.

2. In a large skillet over high heat, heat the vegetable oil for 2 minutes, then lower the heat to medium-high and add the steaks. Cook for 4 minutes, then flip them, add 1 tablespoon of the butter to one side of the skillet, and let the butter melt.

3. With a spoon, scoop up some of the melted butter and spoon it over the steaks, repeat the spooning motion for about 1 minute, then let the steaks cook for 4 minutes (see notes). If you have not trimmed away the fat before cooking, use tongs to hold each steak on its side wherever the fat is and let the fat render for a minute. Remove from the pan and let rest until ready to serve.

4. Lower the heat to medium and pour in the red wine. Deglaze the pan by stirring the wine and loosening any browned bits that are on the bottom, 1 minute. Add the mushrooms and remaining tablespoon of butter and swirl around, then cook, stirring occasionally, for 10 minutes. The liquid will reduce down to a thick sauce.

5. Spoon the mushrooms and sauce over the steaks, then serve and enjoy.

SLOPPY JOE SANDWICHES

Ground Beef
Red Onion
Tomato Soup
Wheat Buns
Pepper Jack
Cheese

MAKES 8 SANDWICHES

These sandwiches are one of my husband's favorites and make for a fantastic quick dinner. They're universally loved and have a very nostalgic taste—they're just plain good all around.

1 pound lean ground beef
½ red onion, finely chopped
1 teaspoon salt
¼ teaspoon freshly ground
   black pepper
1 (10.75-ounce) can
   condensed tomato soup,
   Campbell's preferred
8 wheat hamburger buns (any
   soft bun would work)
8 slices pepper jack cheese

NOTE

The filling of these sandwiches is great for a freezer meal. What I do is make the filling (ground beef, red onion, and condensed tomato soup), let it cool, and then divide it between two resealable plastic freezer bags and freeze it. Then, when we need a quick meal, I simply let the filling thaw in the refrigerator or via the DEFROST *setting in the microwave, and assemble the sandwiches.*

1. In a large skillet, cook the beef and red onion with the salt and pepper, breaking up the beef as it cooks over high heat. Cook until no more pink is visible on the beef, 15 to 20 minutes. It's okay if there is a little bit of grease, but if you want, you can drain it at this point.

2. Stir the condensed tomato soup into the beef mixture. Turn off the heat and stir so that the tomato soup is evenly distributed.

3. Cut the buns in half; place a slice of cheese on each bottom half. Scoop a large spoonful or two of sloppy joe filling onto the cheese, and then place the top bun on top and enjoy.

STUFFED PEPPERS

MAKES 4 STUFFED PEPPERS; SERVES 4

Stuffed peppers are one of my father's favorite dishes. My mother didn't make them because she thought they took too long, so whenever he saw them in delis, he would buy enough to have for dinner and more to freeze. When I was putting together this cookbook, I wanted to find a way to make stuffed peppers faster and easier, and I did just that—it's all about finding a rice medley that takes less than two minutes to make. As soon as I started making these, I realized the genius of freezing them: They reheat oh so well. So, if you're looking for a good make-ahead meal, this is it (they're still really good straight out of the oven).

---

4 bell peppers
1 pound lean ground beef
1 teaspoon salt
¼ teaspoon freshly ground black pepper
1 (8.5-ounce) microwave packet whole-grain medley, brown and wild rice
1 cup shredded marble jack cheese, divided
1 cup sun-dried tomato Alfredo sauce or marinara sauce (see notes)

NOTES

These peppers are good when made with homemade Marinara Sauce (page 219) or Alfredo Sauce (page 213). but I always like to use premade sauce because it keeps the prep time minimal. I like stuffed peppers with a little crunch to them. If you prefer your peppers on the softer side, you can put them in the oven as soon as you preheat it, while you're prepping the filling ingredients, then when the filling is done, remove them from the oven, stuff them, and then return them to the oven.

1. Preheat the oven to 350°F.

2. Cut the tops off the bell peppers and reserve, remove the seeds and innards carefully, and then run a knife across the bottom to take little pieces off (it's as if you're removing the "feet" of them) so that the peppers stand. Place the peppers upright in an 8-inch square baking dish (see notes). Cut the sides of the reserved bell pepper tops into little pieces.

3. In a medium skillet over high heat, combine the beef, salt, black pepper, and little pepper pieces. Cook, stirring occasionally, until the beef browns, about 5 minutes. Remove from the heat, drain if there is liquid in the pan, and transfer to a big bowl.

4. Microwave the grain medley according to the package instructions and add to the cooked beef.

5. Add ¾ cup of the cheese and the sauce. Stir until combined, then stuff each bell pepper with the rice mixture. Sprinkle the remaining ¼ cup of cheese on top of the filling.

6. Bake for 30 minutes, then remove from the oven and allow to cool for a few minutes before serving.

7. If freezing, allow the stuffed peppers to cool completely before wrapping each pepper individually in plastic wrap and then placing in a labeled resealable plastic freezer bag. They will keep in the freezer for up to 3 months.

CHEESY CHICKEN BROCCOLI CASSEROLE

Chicken
Broccoli
Mayonnaise
Cheddar Cheese
Croutons

SERVES 4 (DOUBLES EASILY)

Everyone has a favorite comfort food, and this is my husband's—cheesy chicken and broccoli topped with more cheese and crunchy croutons. It is oh so delicious and is based on a recipe my mother-in-law makes. As soon as the weather starts to cool, this dish is requested over and over.

1½ pounds chicken breast (3 chicken breasts), cut into 1-inch cubes
1 (12-ounce) package steam-in-bag broccoli florets
⅔ cup light mayonnaise
2 cups finely shredded sharp cheddar cheese, divided
1 teaspoon salt
1½ cups croutons, butter and garlic flavor

NOTES

This dish reheats well, so it's perfect for leftover lunches. Try serving this casserole with a little bit of sriracha sauce on top.

1. Preheat the oven to 350°F. Spray a baking dish (I like to use a 9-inch pie dish) with cooking spray.

2. Bring a medium pot of water to a boil, add the cubed chicken, and boil for 10 minutes.

3. While the chicken is cooking, steam the broccoli in the microwave according to the package instructions.

4. In a bowl, combine the mayonnaise and 1 cup of the cheese, and the salt, then stir in the broccoli.

5. When the chicken is done boiling, use a slotted spoon or drain the water and transfer the chicken to the broccoli mixture. Stir a few times, then spoon into the prepared baking dish. Sprinkle the remaining cup of cheese on top and then arrange the croutons evenly atop the chicken mixture. Bake for 15 to 20 minutes, or until the top layer of cheese has melted. Remove from the oven and serve.

CHICKEN FETA TOMATO PASTA

SERVES 4 TO 6

This pasta dish holds a very special place in my heart: When my husband and I first started dating, this was the first meal I ever cooked for him. He still remembers it and whenever I ask him, "What would you like for dinner?" he responds with, "That feta tomato pasta dish." What I love about this dish is that it not only is super delicious, but it's a one-pot meal (yay) for less cleanup.

2 tablespoons extra-virgin olive oil

1½ pounds chicken breast (3 chicken breasts), each breast halved

1 teaspoon salt, divided

¼ teaspoon freshly ground black pepper

2 (14.5-ounce) cans diced tomatoes with basil, garlic, and oregano *=small can*

About 2 cups water

1 pound fettuccine pasta (see note) *= 1 pkg, 375 gm.*

4 ounces feta cheese crumbles, divided

NOTE

I like using fettuccine pasta but any long, straight pasta, such as spaghetti, would work.

1. In a large pot or Dutch oven, heat the olive oil over high heat for 1 minute, then add the chicken breast halves and sprinkle with ½ teaspoon of the salt and the pepper. Cook the chicken for 8 minutes (for a nice crust to form, move it around the pot a little so that it doesn't stick, but don't flip it), lowering the heat a little if you think it is cooking too fast. After 8 minutes, flip it, sprinkle with the remaining ½ teaspoon of salt, then cook the chicken for another 5 minutes.

2. Add the diced tomatoes and the water (I just fill an empty diced tomato can about three-quarters full of water and pour it into the pot; two cans' worth is how much water you need). Stir in the pasta and cook, uncovered, for 5 minutes, then put on the lid and cook for 10 minutes.

3. Remove the lid, stir, and add three-quarters of the cheese crumbles. Stir again and cook, uncovered, for another 5 minutes.

4. Divide among four to six serving bowls, making sure each bowl has an equal amount of chicken and pasta, and then sprinkle the remaining cheese crumbles over the top of the bowls and enjoy.

EASY CHICKEN STIR-FRY

White Rice
Chicken
Olive Oil
Stir-fry Vegetables
Teriyaki Sauce

SERVES 4

Whenever I'm running short on time and need a quick meal (which happens about once a week), I turn to this easy chicken stir-fry. It's super easy to make and you'll have a dinner ready to serve in 30 minutes (prep time included).

---

1 cup uncooked white rice (see notes)

1½ pounds chicken breast (3 chicken breasts), cut into 1-inch cubes (see notes)

1 tablespoon extra-virgin olive oil

½ teaspoon salt

¼ teaspoon freshly ground black pepper

1 (16-ounce) bag frozen stir-fry blend vegetables

1½ cups teriyaki sauce (see notes)

NOTES

I use parboiled white rice, which takes 20 minutes to make. Alternatively, you could use five-minute instant white rice. This dish can be made with your protein of choice: chicken, beef, pork, fish, or tofu. Any teriyaki sauce will work, but one of my favorites is Soy Vay brand Veri Veri Teriyaki Marinade and Sauce.

1. Start by cooking the rice according to the package instructions.

2. Over high heat in a large skillet, sauté the cubed chicken in the olive oil. Sprinkle the chicken with salt and pepper and cook for 10 minutes, then add the frozen vegetables and cook for 3 minutes. Pour in the teriyaki sauce and cook, stirring occasionally, for 5 minutes.

3. Serve over the cooked rice.

LEMON-ROASTED CHICKEN AND POTATOES

SERVES 6

I'm pretty sure my life changed when I found out how easy it was to roast a whole chicken. At first the task seemed daunting, but I decided to just give it a go and I'm so glad I did. Now whenever I need a dinner that has very minimal prep and hands-on time, but that is super delicious, I turn to roasting a chicken. If there are any leftovers (a very seldom occurrence with this dish), you can use the chicken in salads or on sandwiches; the hint of lemon and spices works perfectly for both.

1 whole (5- to 8-pound) chicken, innards removed (see note)
6 medium yellow potatoes, skin on but quartered
¼ cup extra-virgin olive oil
1 tablespoon Mediterranean-spiced sea salt, store-bought of homemade (page 216)
Zest and juice of 1 lemon
1 teaspoon salt

NOTE

You could also make this dish with one and a half pounds of chicken breasts instead of a whole chicken (the cooking time will vary).

1. Preheat the oven to 425°F.

2. Pat the chicken dry with paper towels and place breast side up in a 9 x 13-inch baking dish.

3. Place the potatoes in the dish around the chicken.

4. Drizzle the olive oil over the chicken and potatoes, then sprinkle with the Mediterranean-spiced sea salt, lemon zest, and salt.

5. Bake for 30 minutes, then remove from the oven. Squeeze the lemon juice over the chicken and potatoes and stir the potatoes. Bake for another 20 minutes, or until the juices run clear (the internal temperature of the chicken should be 160° to 170°F on a meat thermometer when done). Let rest for 10 minutes, then slice and serve.

MARINATED YOGURT LEMON CHICKEN

Lemon
Olive Oil
Yogurt
Mediterranean-Spiced
Sea Salt
Chicken

SERVES 4

Whenever I'm not quite sure what I want to make for dinner, this marinated yogurt lemon chicken always comes to mind. I probably make it once every two weeks, and that's coming from the girl who rarely makes the same thing more than once every few months. The yogurt marinade keeps the chicken super moist and the combination of lemon and seasoning really take it to the next level. I also love how versatile this chicken is: You can put it in a pita, use it as a salad topping, or use it as a rice or pasta topper.

Juice of ½ lemon
2 tablespoons extra-virgin
   olive oil
½ cup plain yogurt
1¼ teaspoons Mediterranean-
   spiced sea salt, store-
   bought of homemade (page
   216)
1½ pounds chicken tenders
   (see notes)

NOTES
If you don't have chicken tenders, simply slice chicken breasts into strips (I usually get three or four strips out of one chicken breast). I like making this on the stovetop because the cook time is 10 minutes, but you could also bake it in a baking dish (20 minutes at 400°F).

1. In a bowl, combine the lemon juice, olive oil, yogurt, and Mediterranean-spiced sea salt and stir. Add the chicken tenders and stir so that the chicken is covered in the marinade. Put in refrigerator.

2. Let marinate for 20 minutes (or up to an hour).

3. Heat a large skillet over high heat for 1 minute (see notes), then add the chicken tenders, gently shaking off any excess marinade as you put them in the pan. Discard remaining marinade.

4. Cook for 5 minutes. Drain off the liquid and continue to cook for another 3 minutes. Flip and cook for an additional 3 minutes, or until the chicken is cooked through.

5. Remove from the heat, serve, and enjoy.

ONE-POT CHEESY CHICKEN ENCHILADA PASTA

SERVES 6 TO 8

Who wants to be stuck doing tons of dishes? Not me, that's for sure. With this one-pot recipe you'll have a wonderful meal on the table in less than 30 minutes and cleanup will be a breeze. Everyone will love this twist on chicken enchiladas by having them as a pasta dish. This is definitely one weeknight dinner to make tonight.

1 tablespoon extra-virgin olive oil
½ pound chicken breast tender-
    loins or chicken breast, cubed
¼ teaspoon salt
Pinch of freshly ground black
    pepper
1 (16-ounce) jar red enchilada
    sauce
2 cups water
1 pound pasta (I use gemelli or
    fusilli)
1½ cups Mexican-blend
    shredded cheese

1. In a large pot with a lid, heat the olive oil over high heat for 1 minute, then add the cubed chicken, salt, and pepper. Cook, stirring occasionally, for 8 to 10 minutes, until no more pink is visible and the edges start to brown.

2. Pour the enchilada sauce and water into the pot (see note) and then add the pasta. Stir once, then cover with the lid and let cook, covered, for 5 minutes.

3. Remove the lid, stir, then replace the lid and cook for another 8 minutes. Remove from the heat, stir in the cheese, and serve and enjoy.

NOTE

A cool trick I learned from my mother is that instead of using a measuring cup for pouring the water into the pot, use the empty sauce jar, which holds 2 cups. That way you'll get any remnants of the sauce that remain in the jar and save on cleanup.

PAPRIKA CHICKEN WITH CARROTS & RICE

Brown Rice
Butter
Carrots
Paprika
Chicken

SERVES 4

Paprika was the first spice I remember learning how to cook with. It has a smoky flavor that lends itself really well to chicken and has a beautiful orangey color. Paprika chicken was also one of the first dishes I learned how to cook and to this day is one of my favorite dinners. Served with carrots and over brown rice, this dinner is one to make regularly.

1 cup uncooked brown rice (see notes)

3 tablespoons unsalted butter, divided

5 to 6 large carrots, cut diagonally into large matchsticks

1½ teaspoons paprika, divided

½ teaspoon salt, divided

2 tablespoons water

1½ pounds chicken breast tenderloins (see notes)

¼ teaspoon freshly ground black pepper

NOTES

I like to serve the paprika chicken and carrots over brown rice, but it is also good over egg noodles. In terms of rice, I like to use parboiled instant brown rice—it really reduces the cooking time. If you don't have chicken tenders, you could also use chicken breasts and cut them into strips. I usually get three or four strips per chicken breast.

1. Cook the brown rice according to the package instructions.

2. Meanwhile, in a large skillet, melt 1 tablespoon of the butter and add the carrots. Sprinkle with ½ teaspoon of the paprika and ¼ teaspoon of the salt and sauté for 10 minutes. Add the water and cook for 1 minute, or until the water has reduced down a little, then add the remaining 2 tablespoons of butter and the chicken.

3. Sprinkle the remaining teaspoon of paprika, remaining ¼ teaspoon of salt, and the pepper over the chicken and cook, stirring occasionally, for 20 minutes over medium-high heat, or until the chicken has cooked through and the carrots are tender when poked with a fork.

4. To serve, divide the rice among four plates and top with two to three chicken tenders and some carrots and enjoy.

PESTO AND PEA PASTA WITH CHICKEN

SERVES 3 TO 4

Chicken and pasta are two ingredients that are great for fast and easy cooking, and when combined with a vegetable and pesto, a delicious dinner comes together. For this dish I like to bake the chicken because it reduces hands-on time—all you have to do is pop the chicken in the oven and let it bake away while you make the other components of the dish. When I was growing up, my mother always used to make this dinner for us on busy school nights; it was a great way to get us to eat vegetables and protein while also having something we all loved in it: pasta!

1½ pounds chicken breasts (3 breasts)
1 tablespoon extra-virgin olive oil
½ teaspoon salt
Pinch of freshly ground black pepper
½ pound orecchiette pasta (see notes)
1 (12-ounce) bag frozen peas
3 tablespoons pesto, store-bought or homemade (page 214)

1. Preheat the oven to 350°F. Line a baking dish or sheet with aluminum foil. Place the chicken breasts on the prepared baking dish and drizzle with the olive oil. Sprinkle with salt and pepper and bake for 30 minutes, or until the internal temperature reaches 165°F.

2. While the chicken is baking, bring a large pot of water to a boil. Add the pasta and peas and cook until the pasta is cooked through, about 8 minutes. Drain and return the pasta and peas to the pot. Add the pesto and stir to combine.

3. Divide the pasta and peas among three or four bowls, place a chicken breast on top of each serving (see notes), and serve.

NOTES

You could use any kind of pasta; I like using orecchiette because the little circles scoop up the peas and pesto. If you're feeding smaller stomachs, you could always cut the chicken breasts in half for serving. This meal makes great leftovers, too.

SOUTHERN-STYLE CHICKEN SANDWICHES

Chicken
Pickles
Flour
Butter
Rolls

MAKES 12 SLIDER SANDWICHES

I was introduced to Southern-style chicken sandwiches when I lived in North Carolina. I fell in love with them; they were fried chicken on a bun with a pickle—easy enough, right? I set out to make them and picked up many tips and tricks along the way (such as marinating the chicken in a little pickle juice) and I am so excited to now share this recipe with you (an absolute favorite of my husband's).

---

1 pound chicken breasts
½ cup pickle slices (bread-and-butter pickles work really well), ½ cup pickle juice reserved
¾ cup all-purpose flour
1 teaspoon salt
3 tablespoons unsalted butter
12 sweet slider rolls (I like to use King's Hawaiian brand rolls)

NOTES

Confession: I don't have a meat pounder, so I use any canned good I have in my pantry as a pounder. I wrap the can in plastic wrap, use it to pound the chicken, and when done, throw the plastic wrap away. If you choose, you could also butter your buns, or run them through the pan the chicken has cooked in.

1. Start by prepping the chicken: Cut each chicken breast into quarters, and then place each between two sheets of plastic wrap and pound the chicken to flatten it to ¼ to ½ inch thick (see notes).

2. Pour the pickle juice into a bowl large enough to hold the chicken. Place the flattened chicken pieces in the pickle juice and let sit for 15 minutes (or up to 2 hours in the refrigerator) to marinate.

3. Place the flour in a shallow bowl or on a plate, sprinkle with the salt, and stir a few times.

4. When you're ready to cook the chicken, heat 1 tablespoon of the butter in a skillet over high heat. Dredge one piece of chicken with the flour mixture on both sides, then put it in the skillet. Repeat for the remaining chicken, cooking in batches (I cook four pieces of chicken per batch and do three batches, using 1 tablespoon of butter per batch). Cook the chicken for about 6 minutes per side, flipping only once (that's what gives the chicken its nice golden brown crust; use a meat thermometer to make sure your chicken is cooked through to 165°F).

5. Toast the buns in a toaster or by heating the oven to 350°F and baking them for 5 minutes, or until golden brown (see notes).

6. To assemble, place one piece of chicken on the bottom bun and place one or two pickle slices on top of the chicken, then add the top bun. Repeat to make all the sandwiches, and serve.

"UNFRIED" CORNFLAKE CHICKEN

SERVES 4

Between its crispy, crunchy coating and juicy center, this superdelicious "unfried" chicken will have you questioning your once devotion to its opposite: fried chicken. This chicken is one of the dishes I'm known for, something I make for all my friends, and what I make when I need a dish that is universally loved. It goes great with a side of Mashed Potatoes (page 71) or as a salad topping.

1½ pounds chicken breast
   tenderloins (see notes)
1 cup milk
3 tablespoons unsalted butter,
   melted
2 cups cornflakes
2 tablespoons paprika
½ teaspoon salt
Pinch of freshly ground black
   pepper

NOTES

You can cut regular chicken breasts into strips if you don't have chicken tenders. I usually get three or four strips per chicken breast, but if you're looking for a time-saving tip, get tenders; then you don't have to worry about cutting them up. Another time-saving tip: You can make the cornflake topping beforehand and freeze it. I'll sometimes make a double batch of it and then store it in the freezer until I'm ready to use it.

1. Place the chicken tenders in a medium to large bowl, pour in the milk so that it covers the chicken, and let it sit for 20 minutes (or cover and refrigerate overnight).

2. Preheat the oven to 425°F.

3. In a small bowl, melt the butter (I do so by microwaving it for 30 seconds on HIGH). Spoon about half of the butter onto the bottom of a 9 x 13-inch Pyrex or foil-lined baking dish and set aside.

4. Pour the cornflakes, paprika, salt, and pepper into a food processor and process for 5 seconds, or until most of the cornflakes are crushed but a few bigger pieces still remain. Alternatively, you could put the mixture in a bag and crush it between two plates or by running a canned good over it—you just want to turn it into a crushed topping, whichever way is easiest. Pour the topping mixture into a shallow bowl (see notes).

5. Now, take one chicken tender at a time out of the milk mixture, lightly tap off any excess milk, and place it in the topping bowl. Spoon the topping over both sides of the chicken, pressing the topping to any parts that are not coated, then place in the prepared baking dish. Repeat until all the chicken is coated and in the baking dish.

6. Drizzle the remaining melted butter over the chicken and bake for 10 minutes, then remove from the oven, flip the chicken strips, and bake for another 10 minutes. Remove from the oven, allow to cool for a few minutes, and enjoy.

YOGURT CHICKEN AND CARAMELIZED ONION PASTA

SERVES 4

There's something irresistible about this pasta dish to me. The onion caramelizes and combines with the yogurt to make a rich and creamy sauce for pasta. Topped with chicken it is an all-around delicious meal.

1 large red onion, finely sliced
3 tablespoons extra-virgin
    olive oil, divided
1 pound chicken breast, each
    breast cut into thirds, or
    chicken tenders (see note)
Pinch each of salt and freshly
    ground black pepper
8 ounces fettuccine pasta
1 cup plain yogurt

NOTE
To cook the chicken faster, cut it into 1-inch cubes.

1. In a large skillet over medium heat, cook the red onion in 2 tablespoons of the olive oil, stirring occasionally, for 20 minutes, or until the onion is soft and caramelized. Add the remaining tablespoon of olive oil and the chicken, and sprinkle with a pinch of salt and pepper. Cook for 15 minutes, or until the chicken is cooked through, and remove from the heat.

2. Meanwhile, cook the pasta according to the package instructions. Drain, reserving ½ cup of the cooking water, and return the pasta to the pot it was cooked in. Pour the reserved water back into the pot with the pasta, and stir in the yogurt until the noodles are coated with the yogurt.

3. Add the chicken mixture to the pasta, stir, and serve.

BRAT AND CARAMELIZED ONION PIZZA

MAKES 1 PIZZA; SERVES 8

The flavors of this pizza are based on a tradition that takes place in the city I live in, Milwaukee. That tradition is tailgating. I had been to some tailgates before, but here in Milwaukee (as in the state of Wisconsin), they're truly next level. People arrive hours before the game and grill and cook out. And typical of tailgates are brats. One day I was thinking of different fun game day foods and came up with this recipe. Whenever we have friends coming over to watch a game (or on his birthday), my husband always requests I make this pizza!

1½ tablespoons unsalted butter, divided
½ onion, finely sliced
½ teaspoon salt
2 uncooked bratwursts (see note)
1 premade thin pizza crust
8 ounces fresh mozzarella cheese, sliced

NOTE

You can use any kind of brats. I like to buy "beer brats," which are made with real beer.

1. Preheat the oven to 400°F.

2. In a medium skillet over high heat, melt 1 tablespoon of the butter and then add the onion and salt. Cook, stirring occasionally, for 13 to 15 minutes, or until the onion is caramelized (reduce the heat if it starts to brown).

3. In a small skillet, melt the remaining ½ tablespoon of butter and add the brats. Cook for 5 minutes, then flip and cook for another 5 minutes. Remove from the pan and cut each brat into little pieces (I just cut them in the pan).

4. Lay the pizza crust on a pizza baking sheet and arrange the cheese on top of the crust.

5. Sprinkle the cooked brat slices and caramelized onion over the cheese and then bake for 14 minutes.

6. Remove from the oven, allow to cool for a few minutes, then slice and enjoy.

CRUSTED PORK CHOPS & GREEN BEANS

Olive Oil
Pork Chops
Dijon Mustard
Panko Bread Crumbs
Green Beans

SERVES 4

Breaded with Italian-seasoned, Japanese-style bread crumbs, these pork chops are super flavorful and a fantastic easy meal for a weeknight dinner. I heard from my husband that while he was growing up, his mother used to make the same protein on certain nights of the week (I love that idea!). Thursday was pork chop night, so here is one of my favorite ways to enjoy pork chops—with a little tang from the mustard and a crispy crust, served alongside green beans. Perfect for pork chop night.

2 tablespoons extra-virgin olive oil
1½ pounds pork chops (4 pork chops)
2 teaspoons Dijon mustard
¼ cup Italian-style panko bread crumbs (see notes)
¼ teaspoon salt
¼ teaspoon freshly ground black pepper
1 (16-ounce) bag frozen French-style green beans

NOTES
You could substitute Italian-style bread crumbs for the panko bread crumbs, but while it still tastes delicious, it doesn't have quite the same crispy crust that forms when you use panko. Panko can be found right next to regular bread crumbs in major grocery stores. The internal temperature for pork chop doneness is 145° to 160°F.

1. In a large skillet, heat the olive oil over high heat for 2 minutes.

2. Meanwhile, pat the pork chops dry with a paper towel and set on a plate. Spread the chops with about ½ teaspoon of mustard per side, then sprinkle about 1½ teaspoons of bread crumbs per side, pressing the crumbs into the mustard so that they stick. Place the chops in the skillet and sprinkle with salt and pepper.

3. Cook the pork chops for 5 minutes per side, only flipping once so that a nice crust forms on each side. After cooking for 10 minutes (see notes), turn off the heat and let the chops sit in the pan for 5 minutes; this will keep them nice and juicy while you're heating your green beans.

4. Heat the green beans according to the package instructions.

5. To serve, place one crispy, crusted pork chop on each plate alongside a quarter of the green beans and enjoy.

FORBIDDEN RICE BOWL

Butter
Black Forbidden Rice
Bacon
Kale
Parmesan Cheese

SERVES 2 TO 3

Black rice—also known as forbidden rice—is deep purple (it looks black, hence the name) but otherwise is similar to Thai jasmine rice or brown rice. It is slightly nutty in taste and goes perfectly with crispy bacon, kale, and Parmesan cheese. Give me a rice bowl for dinner any night and I'm a happy girl. As a matter of fact, I'm not the only one in my house that loves these rice bowls. After coming home from a business trip, my husband said he had missed my rice bowl creations for dinner. Thirty minutes later, I had remedied that. These bowls are super easy to prepare and are great for a quick weeknight meal.

1¾ cups water
1 tablespoon unsalted butter
1 teaspoon salt
1 cup uncooked black forbidden rice (see notes)
½ pound thick-cut bacon (6 to 8 slices), cut into 1-inch pieces
1 bunch kale, stemmed and chopped (about 1½ cups chopped)
⅓ cup shaved or finely grated Parmesan cheese (see notes)

1. In a medium pot with a lid, bring the water, butter, and salt to a boil. Add the rice, lower the heat to low, cover, and cook until the rice has absorbed the water, 25 to 30 minutes.

2. Meanwhile, in a large skillet, fry the bacon pieces, stirring occasionally, for 10 minutes. When the bacon is almost done cooking, add the kale and cook for 5 minutes, until the kale has softened.

3. To assemble the bowls, divide the rice among your bowls, make a little well in the middle, spoon the kale mixture into the well, and then top with the cheese and enjoy.

NOTES

Black forbidden rice is sold at most major grocery stores in the rice aisle, at natural food stores, and on Amazon.com. If you don't have black rice, you could replace it with brown rice (cooking times vary). Use a Microplane to grate the Parmesan cheese for superfine little cheese curls as in the picture.

ITALIAN SAUSAGE PARMESAN RIGATONI

Rigatoni
Olive Oil
Italian Sausage
Marinara Sauce
Parmesan Cheese

SERVES 4 TO 6

This dish was a staple in our household on busy weeknights when I was growing up; it's such a super simple meal to make and one that everyone loves. Pasta is topped with a thick meat red sauce and then is topped with Parmesan; it's delicious and ready in 20 minutes.

1 pound rigatoni pasta
1 tablespoon extra-virgin olive oil
1½ pounds casing-free Italian sausage (see note)
½ teaspoon salt
1 (24-ounce) jar marinara sauce, or homemade (page 219)
½ cup grated Parmesan cheese

NOTE

I like to buy fresh Italian sausage from the meat counter, but I've also made this dish with turkey Italian sausage sold in casings and removed the casings.

1. In a large pot, cook the pasta according to the package instructions. Drain and set aside.

2. In a large skillet over high heat, heat the olive oil for 30 seconds, then add the sausage and salt. Cook, breaking up the meat as it cooks, for 10 to 15 minutes, or until no more pink is visible.

3. Pour the marinara sauce into the meat, stir, and cook for 2 minutes.

4. To serve, divide the pasta among four to six bowls and top with a ladleful or two of the meat sauce, sprinkle the cheese on top, and serve.

PROSCIUTTO PARMESAN QUICHE

MAKES 1 LARGE PIE; SERVES 8

This light and fluffy quiche makes for a delicious meal at any time of the day (quiche can be enjoyed for breakfast, lunch, or dinner). When I was growing up, quiche was always served on Sundays or when guests came over because it has a superquick prep time and then it could bake in the oven while we were spending time with family and friends.

---

1 premade (9-inch) deep-dish
  piecrust
5 large eggs
1 cup heavy cream
1 teaspoon salt
1 (5.29-ounce) package sliced
  prosciutto
1 cup shredded Parmesan,
  Swiss, or Cheddar cheese

1. Preheat the oven to 375°F. Place the piecrust on a baking sheet and set aside.

2. In a bowl, whisk together the eggs, cream, and salt until well combined.

3. Add the prosciutto and cheese and then whisk a few times, until the ingredients are combined.

4. Pour the egg mixture into the piecrust and bake for 40 to 45 minutes, or until the top is golden brown. The quiche will puff up. Remove from the oven and allow to cool for 5 minutes (it will set). Slice and serve.

SODA PULLED PORK

Pork Shoulder
Red Onion
Cola Soda

MAKES 4 TO 5 POUNDS PULLED PORK

This is one of the tastiest (and easiest) pulled pork recipes ever. I've made this time and time again, and the pork always comes out juicy and moist with a subtle sweetness that is second to none. Simply put all ingredients in your slow cooker and set it and forget it. You'll come back to perfectly cooked pork that can be shredded in minutes.

1 (3½- to 4½-pound) pork shoulder
2 teaspoons salt
½ teaspoon freshly ground black pepper
1 large red onion, sliced (optional)
3 cups full-flavored cola soda, such as Coke or Pepsi

NOTES

This pork is great in tacos (see the Pork Carnitas Tacos, page 138, which uses this recipe) or on sandwiches with some BBQ sauce or as a nacho topping (see page 64 for a nachos recipe).

1. Place the pork shoulder, fat side down, in a slow cooker. Sprinkle with the salt and pepper.

2. Place the red onion in the slow cooker around the pork.

3. Pour the soda over the pork. Cover the slow cooker and set on LOW. Cook for 8 hours, then transfer the pork to a shallow bowl or cutting board with a lip and, using two forks, shred it.

4. To store, place the shredded pork in an airtight container and pour some juices from the slow cooker over the meat. This pork freezes and reheats very well. To freeze, place the shredded pork in a resealable plastic freezer bag and label with the date when it was made.

PORK CARNITAS TACOS

MAKES 20 TO 24 TACOS; SERVES 12 (SEE NOTES)

Taco Tuesdays, anyone? I love the alliterations, especially involving food—Taco Tuesdays, Five-Ingredient Fridays—so it's no surprise that I love these tacos and tend to enjoy them on Tuesdays and Fridays (Fiesta Fridays or Five-Ingredient Fridays apply in the latter case). These tacos are super simple and super flavorful: Juicy pulled pork is topped with cilantro and lime and then served in tortillas; it makes for one delicious dinner.

24 small tortilla shells (corn tortilla shells work great)
1 recipe Soda Pulled Pork (page 137; see notes)
1 cup chopped fresh cilantro (from 1 bunch cilantro)
4 limes, sliced into wedges, for serving

NOTES

This recipe is easily scaled down: Simply make as many tacos as desired and save the remaining pork and tacos for leftovers. When I expect to make Pork Carnitas Tacos, I typically don't add the red onion when cooking the pork.

1. Preheat the oven to 350°F. Place the tortillas on a baking sheet and bake for 3 to 5 minutes, or until the edges start to curl up. Remove from the oven and set on a plate.

2. Put the shredded pork, cilantro, and lime wedges in individual bowls for taco assembly.

3. To assemble the tacos, put a few forkfuls of pork into a tortilla shell, add a pinch of cilantro, and squeeze some lime juice on top. Repeat until all the tacos are assembled, then serve and enjoy.

TORTELLINI AND SAUSAGE BAKE

Tortellini
Olive Oil
Sausage
Marinara Sauce
Mozzarella Cheese

SERVES 6 TO 8

This comfort dish is packed with lots of cheese: a cheese filling of tortellini, cheese in the sausage, and then cheese melted on top. It makes for a delicious dinner.

---

2 (8-ounce) packages dried or fresh four-cheese tortellini pasta

1 tablespoon extra-virgin olive oil

1 pound sausage, cut into pieces (see note)

1 (24-ounce) jar marinara sauce, roasted garlic flavor

1 cup shredded low-moisture, part-skim mozzarella cheese

NOTE

I usually buy chicken or turkey sausage; any sausage will work for this dish. My favorite is garlic and mozzarella chicken sausage.

---

1. Preheat the oven to 375°F.

2. Cook the tortellini according to the package instructions (about 10 minutes for dried, quicker for fresh). When they're almost done (al dente), remove from the heat and drain.

3. Heat the olive oil in a skillet and fry the sausage pieces over high heat, stirring occasionally, to brown them slightly, 5 minutes.

4. Pour the tortellini into a 9 x 12-inch baking dish and then put the cooked sausage pieces on top. Next, pour the marinara sauce on top and sprinkle with the cheese. Bake for 15 minutes, or until the cheese is golden brown.

5. Remove from the oven, allow to cool for 5 minutes, and serve.

Ground Turkey
Panko Bread Crumbs
Sour Cream
Olive Oil
Marinara Sauce

THE BEST TURKEY MEAT SAUCE

SERVES 6

I love using ground turkey for this amazing meat sauce; it is thick and has a slightly creamy texture. It truly is the best turkey meat sauce. It can be used as a topping for pasta or rice and can even be made into meatballs (see note).

1 pound ground turkey
¼ cup Italian-style panko bread crumbs
½ cup sour cream
¼ teaspoon salt
1 tablespoon extra-virgin olive oil
1 (24-ounce) jar marinara sauce, tomato and basil flavor, store-bought or homemade (page 219)

1. In a large bowl, combine the turkey, bread crumbs, sour cream, and salt and mix well.

2. Over high heat, heat the olive oil in a large skillet for 30 seconds, then add the turkey mixture. Cook, breaking it up as it browns, for 10 minutes, then add the marinara sauce and cook for 5 more minutes.

3. Serve over pasta or rice and enjoy.

NOTES
To make into meatballs, add an additional ½ cup of panko bread crumbs and form into meatballs. Cook them whole in the olive oil instead of breaking them up as they brown.

SOY SAUCE SHRIMP AND GRITS

Yellow Cornmeal
Butter
Parmigiano-Reggiano Cheese
Shrimp
Soy Sauce

SERVES 4

This is one flavorful dinner, inspired by my time spent living in the South (North Carolina), where I found a love for grits. If you've never had grits, or only have had them at a restaurant, I urge you to try this recipe. Grits are super easy to make and are amazing when topped with shrimp, plus this whole meal only takes 20 minutes to cook, which makes it perfect for a quick weeknight meal.

FOR THE GRITS:
4½ cups water, divided
1 teaspoon salt
1 cup yellow cornmeal
3 tablespoons unsalted butter
½ cup shredded Parmigiano-Reggiano, Parmesan, or cheddar cheese

FOR THE SHRIMP:
1 tablespoon unsalted butter
1 pound raw shrimp (see note)
½ teaspoon salt
2 tablespoons soy sauce

NOTE

I like to get frozen raw large shrimp (1 pound per bag) that are peeled, deveined, and tail on—it makes prep a breeze. If buying them from the fishmonger at your grocery store, ask whether the store's frozen raw shrimp are like that, and if not, the fishmonger will usually offer to peel and devein them for you.

1. **Make the grits:** In a large pot, combine 3½ cups of the water and the salt and bring to a boil. In a bowl, combine the remaining cup of water and the cornmeal. When the water comes to a boil, whisk in the cornmeal mixture. Bring to a boil again and then lower the heat to low. The mixture will thicken slowly. Five minutes after lowering the heat, whisk in the butter and cheese. This is the point when I start the shrimp. The grits should remain on low heat, whisked occasionally, for the next 10 minutes, then the heat can be turned off and they can rest until they are ready to be served.

2. **Make the shrimp:** In a skillet, melt the butter. Add the shrimp and cook for 2 minutes, stirring occasionally, then sprinkle in the salt and pour in the soy sauce. Cook for 8 minutes, or until the shrimp are no longer translucent and turn pink.

3. To serve, spoon the grits into four bowls and top with the shrimp.

Salmon
Butternut Squash
Cherry Tomatoes
Olive Oil
Lemon

SUNRISE SALMON

SERVES 4

This dish is named for all its vibrant colors; it makes me think of a beautiful sunrise. I love finding cherry tomatoes that are varying colors of red and orange. This simple recipe makes for a delicious dinner that comes together in a flash.

1 (16- to 20-ounce) salmon fillet
12 ounces butternut squash, cubed (about 2 cups; see note)
1 cup cherry tomatoes
2 tablespoons extra-virgin olive oil
1 teaspoon salt
¼ teaspoon freshly ground black pepper
1 lemon, finely sliced

NOTE

I like buying butternut squash that has already been cubed because it really reduces prep time. You can find it in the produce section of most grocery stores, or you could buy frozen cut butternut squash.

1. Preheat the oven to 350°F. Line a baking sheet with aluminum foil.

2. Lay the salmon fillet, skin side down, on a baking sheet and pat dry with a piece of paper towel.

3. Place the butternut squash pieces and cherry tomatoes around the salmon. Drizzle the olive oil over the salmon and vegetables.

4. Sprinkle the salt and pepper over the salmon and vegetables, then lay the lemon slices over the salmon and bake for 30 minutes. Turn off the heat and leave the pan in the oven for 5 minutes, then remove the pan from the oven and enjoy.

TILAPIA TACOS

Olive Oil
Tilapia
Taco Seasoning
Mexican Corn Blend Frozen Vegetables
Tortillas

SERVES 4

These tacos are perfect for a light dinner when you're looking for a superquick meal; they take 15 minutes to make and have great flavors. It was actually my husband who, years ago, suggested this flavor combination of tilapia on tacos and I've been making them ever since, because we love what an easy dinner they are to make.

1 tablespoon extra-virgin olive oil
10 ounces tilapia fillets
  (4 fillets)
1 tablespoon taco seasoning,
  store-bought or homemade
  (page 216), divided
1 (12-ounce) package steam-
  in-bag frozen fire-roasted
  Mexican corn blend (see
  notes)
8 tortilla shells

NOTES

*Any frozen corn blend would
work; one with southwestern
flavors is always good.*

1. In a large skillet over high heat, heat the olive oil for 1 minute, then add the tilapia fillets and sprinkle a pinch of taco seasoning on each of the fillets. Cook for 3 minutes, then flip and cook for another 3 minutes, sprinkling with the remaining taco seasoning. There should be no more translucent parts to the tilapia when it is done; I usually cut one of the fillets in half to check for doneness.

2. While the fish cooks, heat the frozen vegetables according to the package instructions and warm the tortillas (I do so by heating them in a 350°F oven for 3 minutes).

3. To assemble the tacos, place ½ tilapia fillet in a tortilla and spoon the corn mixture on top, then serve and enjoy.

Ramen Noodles

Frozen Mixed
Vegetables

Butter

Parmesan Cheese

Egg

RAMEN WITH FRIED EGG

SERVES 1 (RECIPE EASILY MULTIPLIES)

Whenever I have superlate days at work and am so exhausted when I get home that I can't even think of ordering delivery because it will take too long, this is the recipe I make. It takes whopping 15 minutes from start to finish and is just a fantastic recipe that I have been making for years. Ever since college, years ago, I seem to always keep a few packets of ramen noodles in my pantry. I think it was back then that I realized the magic of ramen. It is a noodle dish but it doesn't have to be a brothy soup. I transform it into a delicious pasta dish and top it with a sunny-side up egg. When you poke the yolk over the noodles and stir it, it becomes like a ramen carbonara. This dish is so good, it's a must-try.

1 (3-ounce) package chicken-flavor ramen (or flavor of your choice)

⅔ cup frozen mixed vegetables

1 tablespoon salted or unsalted butter, divided

2 tablespoons shredded Parmesan cheese

1 large egg

Pinch each of salt and freshly ground black pepper

1. Fill a small pot about halfway up with water and bring to a boil over high heat.

2. Remove the seasoning packet from the ramen and set aside. Add the dried ramen noodles and frozen vegetables to the boiling water. Allow to boil for 3 to 5 minutes, or until the noodles break up easily when poked with a fork.

3. Drain the water from the noodles and vegetables and return them to the pot. Sprinkle the contents of the seasoning packet over the noodles and vegetables and add ½ tablespoon of the butter and all of the cheese. Stir until well combined and the butter has melted.

4. Meanwhile, melt the remaining ½ tablespoon of butter in a small skillet over high heat. Crack in the egg and sprinkle with the salt and pepper. Cook over high heat for 1 minute and then lower the heat to medium. Cook for 4 minutes (this is for a sunny-side up egg; if you like your eggs cooked longer, do so).

5. To serve, place the noodle mixture in a big bowl, top with the egg, and enjoy.

SPINACH ALFREDO LASAGNE

Alfredo Sauce
Lasagna Noodles
Spinach
Ricotta Cheese
Italian Blend
Shredded Cheese

SERVES 12

Perfect for family dinners, this white lasagne feeds a crowd and is full of cheesy deliciousness. Have vegetarians in your family? This would also be perfect for them, or it would be great for a Meatless Monday dish.

1 (15-ounce) jar creamy Alfredo sauce, store-bought or homemade (page 213), divided

1 (9-ounce) package oven-ready lasagna noodles

1 (24-ounce) package frozen chopped spinach

1 (15-ounce) container part-skim ricotta cheese

2 teaspoons salt

2 cups Italian blend shredded cheese, or shredded plain low-moisture, part-skim mozzarella

NOTE

Lasagne is one of those dishes that freezes and then subsequently reheats really well, so this would make an excellent dish to have on hand in the freezer or to gift someone as a freezer meal. I like to use disposable baking dishes so that if I bring this to someone's house, I can just leave the pan and cleanup is a breeze.

1. Preheat the oven to 375°F.

2. Spread ¼ cup of the Alfredo sauce on the bottom of a 9 x 13-inch baking dish (see note). Place a layer of noodles down on top of the sauce. If the noodles don't fit, break them up to create an even layer.

3. Microwave the spinach in a microwave-safe bowl, 5 minutes on HIGH, and drain away the liquid. Mix in the ricotta cheese and salt.

4. Spoon half of the spinach mixture into a layer on top of the noodles, sprinkle with a handful of the shredded cheese, then lay another layer of noodles on top.

5. Spread remaining half of the spinach mixture on top, then sprinkle a little bit of shredded cheese and a few spoonfuls (4 to 5 tablespoons) of Alfredo sauce on top.

6. Lay another layer of noodles on top, and spoon the remaining Alfredo sauce on top.

7. Fill the empty sauce jar one-quarter full with water (about ½ cup) and pour on top of the noodles. Spread around so that the sauce is distributed evenly, then sprinkle the remaining shredded cheese on top. Bake for 50 minutes, or until the cheese is browned and bubbly on the top around the edges. Allow to cool for 15 minutes, slice into 12 pieces, and enjoy.

TOFU STIR-FRY WITH PEANUT SAUCE

SERVES 4

Stir-frying is fantastic for quick and easy meals. Tofu is also great because it takes mere minutes to cook. If you've never tried tofu, I urge you to try it with this stir-fry; it's cooked in a delicious peanut butter sauce and tastes super good. I never thought I'd say this, but my husband actually requests this tofu stir-fry because it's so delicious.

½ cup soy sauce
¼ cup creamy peanut butter
1 (12-ounce) package extra-firm tofu (see note)
1 tablespoon vegetable oil
½ teaspoon salt
1 (16-ounce) bag frozen stir-fry blend vegetables

NOTE

The beauty of this recipe is that it can be made with the protein of your choice: tofu, chicken, pork, or beef. Serve over rice.

1. In a bowl, whisk together the soy sauce and peanut butter and set aside. There may be some clumpy bits, but that's okay; they will cook and melt together.

2. Drain the tofu and pat dry with a paper towel, then cut into 1-inch cubes.

3. In a large skillet, heat the vegetable oil over high heat for 1 minute, then add the tofu cubes and sprinkle with the salt. Cook for 1 minute, then add ¼ cup of the peanut butter mixture and cook for 4 minutes, flipping occasionally.

4. Remove the tofu from the pan and transfer to a plate.

5. Add the remaining ½ cup of the peanut butter mixture to the pan and whisk until smooth, then add the frozen vegetables and cook for 5 minutes, or until the vegetables are cooked through. Return the tofu to the pan, stir, and serve and enjoy.

ZITI PASTA BAKE

SERVES 6 TO 8

Ziti
Marinara Sauce
Ricotta Cheese
Parmesan Cheese
Mozzarella Cheese

Ziti has always been one of my favorite Italian dishes. Pasta covered in cheese in a creamy ricotta and marinara sauce mixture with more cheese? Sign me up! It's no wonder that ziti is a family favorite recipe, too, with kids and adults alike loving it. Now you can make it for family dinner and be everyone's favorite cook.

16 ounces ziti pasta

1 (24-ounce) jar marinara sauce, tomato-basil-garlic flavor, store-bought or homemade (page 219)

1 (15-ounce) container ricotta cheese, divided

½ cup grated Parmesan cheese

2 cups shredded low-moisture, part-skim mozzarella cheese

Note
This goes great with a side of Cheesy Garlic Bread (page 57).

1. Preheat the oven to 350°F.

2. Cook the ziti according to the package instructions. Drain the water, return the pasta to the pot, pour in the marinara sauce, and stir.

3. Drop about three-quarters of the ricotta cheese by the spoonful into the pot. Sprinkle the Parmesan cheese into the pot and gently stir.

4. Pour the contents of the pot into a 9 x 13-inch baking dish and spoon the remaining ricotta cheese onto the ziti mixture, nestling it in so that the ziti is covering it.

5. Sprinkle the mozzarella cheese on top of the ziti mixture and bake for 25 minutes, or until the cheese is melted and starts to turn golden brown around the edges. Remove from the oven, then serve and enjoy.

SWEETS
AND
TREATS

BROWNIE BITES

Chocolate
Butter
Sugar
Eggs
Flour

MAKES 24 MINI BROWNIES

Brownies are my favorite dessert of all time. It just doesn't get any better than rich mini brownie bites. These are a huge hit for parties or anytime you are in need of a brownie fix.

10 ounces semisweet baking chocolate or 1½ cups semisweet chocolate chips; (see notes)
½ cup (1 stick; 4 ounces) unsalted butter
¾ cup sugar
2 large eggs
1 cup all-purpose flour

NOTES

I have found the best results with using a high-quality chocolate, such as Ghirardelli brand chocolate chips or Baker's brand baking squares. If you don't have a mini muffin pan, you could bake the batter in an 8-inch square baking pan for 40 minutes at 350°F and then cut them into brownies.

1. Preheat the oven to 350°F. Spray a 24-cup mini muffin pan with cooking spray (see notes).

2. In a microwave-safe bowl, microwave the chocolate and butter for 30 seconds on HIGH. Then remove from the microwave and stir. Repeat, microwaving for 30 seconds and stirring, until the chocolate mixture is smooth and creamy (mine usually takes 1½ minutes, or three intervals of heating).

3. Carefully stir in the sugar with a spoon (no need to use a mixer).

4. When the sugar is incorporated, add the eggs and stir until combined, then mix in the flour and stir until combined. No big lumps should remain.

5. Using a tablespoon-size cookie scoop or spoon, fill each muffin cup with a heaping tablespoon of brownie batter. Bake for 14 minutes.

6. Remove from the oven and allow to cool for at least 30 minutes, then gently remove the brownie bites from the muffin pan by running a sharp knife tip around the edges to loosen any parts that may have stuck, and serve.

BUTTERSCOTCH CORNFLAKE CLUSTERS

**Butterscotch Chips
Cornflakes**

MAKES 24 TO 26 CLUSTERS

Around the holidays there were four or five cookies we would always make and arrange on platters to give to friends and family. These clusters always made the list because they are super easy to make and are a no-bake recipe. I've kept alive the tradition of making them around the holidays because, well, they are so good and so incredibly simple, with literally two ingredients. They make the perfect addition to any holiday cookie tray, and are also great to bring along to parties.

---

1 (11-ounce) bag butterscotch
  chips
4 cups cornflakes

1. Line two baking sheets with parchment paper (or just roll out parchment paper and set it on an empty counter or flat surface).

2. Microwave the butterscotch chips in a large microwave-safe bowl for 30 seconds on HIGH. Then remove from the microwave and stir. Repeat, microwaving for 30 seconds and stirring, until the butterscotch is smooth and creamy (mine takes 2 minutes, or four intervals of heating).

3. Carefully stir in the cornflakes until they are coated with butterscotch.

4. Using a tablespoon-size cookie scoop or spoon, scoop a tablespoonful of the mixture onto the prepared parchment paper. Repeat until all the clusters have been formed. You don't need to leave a lot of space between them because you're not baking them; you just don't want them to touch.

5. Allow the clusters to cool for about an hour (or until they have set), and transfer to a tin or serving plate and enjoy.

CANDY BAR CHEESECAKE COOKIES

Cream Cheese
Butter
Sugar
Flour
Snickers Bars

MAKES 24 COOKIES

Cookies in the freezer? Why, yes! These cookies come out best when the dough is frozen and then baked, so what I like to do is whip up a batch to keep in the freezer so that when we have unexpected guests or I feel like a cookie (or two), I can simply remove them from the freezer and bake them.

4 ounces cream cheese, softened
½ cup (1 stick; 4 ounces) unsalted butter, at room temperature
¾ cup sugar
1 cup all-purpose flour
4 Snickers candy bars, cut into little pieces

1. Preheat the oven to 350°F. Line a baking sheet with a silicone baking mat or parchment paper.

2. In a bowl, using a hand (or stand) mixer, beat the cream cheese and butter together until fluffy, about 2 minutes, then scrape down the sides of the bowl with a spatula. Add the sugar and mix until well combined.

3. Add the flour and mix to combine (the dough will be slightly crumbly but very soft to the touch). With a wooden spoon, gently fold in the Snickers pieces and stir to combine.

4. With a tablespoon-size cookie scoop, scoop 1-tablespoon dough balls (or form and roll the balls of dough with your fingers) and place them onto the prepared cookie sheet. There doesn't have to be too much room between them because you're just freezing them. Flatten the cookies slightly with the back of a spoon or a spatula.

5. Place the cookie sheet in the freezer for an hour. You can remove the cookie sheet from the freezer and bake the cookies at this point, or you can remove the frozen cookie balls from the cookie sheet, put them in a resealable plastic freezer bag, and keep them in the freezer until you're ready to bake them.

6. To bake, preheat the oven to 350°F. Line two baking sheets with a silicone baking mat or parchment paper. Place the frozen cookie dough 2 inches apart on the prepared baking sheets.

7. Bake for 10 to 12 minutes, remove from the oven (the cookies will be soft, which is exactly what you want), cool on the pans for at least 5 minutes, transfer to a cooling rack, and enjoy.

Chocolate
Sweetened Condensed Milk
Vanilla Extract
Cocoa Powder
Graham Crackers

GRAHAM CRACKER COOKIE TRUFFLES

MAKES ABOUT 40 TRUFFLES

Graham crackers combine with chocolate to form these rich cookie truffles. They taste like cookie balls and are a fun sweet treat to serve at parties.

8 ounces semisweet chocolate or 1¼ cups semisweet chocolate chips
1 (14-ounce) can sweetened condensed milk
1 teaspoon pure vanilla extract
1 tablespoon unsweetened cocoa powder, plus about 2 tablespoons for rolling (see notes)
2½ cups crushed graham cracker crumbs (see notes)

NOTE

If you don't like the bitter taste of unsweetened cocoa on truffles, you can use sweetened cocoa powder for rolling instead. I crush my graham crackers by pulsating them in the food processor, but you could also buy them precrushed (as for piecrusts), which really cuts down prep time. After the initial cooling, you can remove the truffles from the fridge and store at room temperature.

1. Microwave the chocolate in a microwave-safe bowl for 30 seconds on HIGH. Remove from the microwave and stir. Repeat, microwaving for 30 seconds and stirring, until the chocolate has melted (usually takes 2 minutes, or four intervals of heating).

2. Slowly pour the condensed milk into the melted chocolate. Stir to combine, add the vanilla, and stir.

3. Stir in the 1 tablespoon of cocoa powder and the crushed graham cracker crumbs and stir until the batter is thick and all the ingredients are mixed together.

4. Place the remaining 2 tablespoons of cocoa powder in a shallow bowl.

5. With a tablespoon-size cookie scoop, scoop 1 tablespoon of batter into your hands and roll to form a 1-inch ball. Roll the ball in the cocoa powder to coat. Place in a little wrapper, or just set on a plate, and repeat until all the batter has been formed into balls. Refrigerate for an hour (or overnight) to set the truffles, and serve.

PEANUT BUTTER SEA SALT COOKIES

Brown Sugar
Eggs
Vanilla Extract
Peanut Butter
Sea Salt

MAKES 30 COOKIES

All hail the glorious peanut butter cookie. This is one of my all-time favorite cookie recipes: a sweet, flourless peanut butter cookie with a slightly chewy center, topped with a hint of sea salt. It is simply amazing.

- 2 cups packed light brown sugar
- 2 large eggs, at room temperature
- 1 teaspoon pure vanilla extract
- 2 cups creamy peanut butter (see notes)
- 1 tablespoon sea salt, for garnish (optional)

NOTES

I always use Skippy brand creamy peanut butter, I've found that it is the most consistent in terms of baking with and providing the perfect flavor. Whenever I make these cookies and bring them over to my in-laws, they always make peanut butter ice-cream sandwiches by using one scoop of vanilla ice cream pressed between two cookies.

1. Preheat the oven to 350°F. Line two baking sheets with parchment paper or silicone baking mats and set aside.

2. In a bowl, whisk together the brown sugar and eggs, then whisk in the vanilla.

3. With a wooden spoon, stir in the peanut butter until a thick and creamy batter forms; it is ready when no plain peanut butter can be seen and all the ingredients are incorporated.

4. With a tablespoon-size cookie scoop or spoon, form 1-tablespoon dough balls and place them on the prepared cookie sheets. Bake for 10 minutes, or until the edges are slightly browned (it's okay if they crack). Remove from the oven, sprinkle a little sea salt over the cookies, and pat down slightly with the back of a flat spatula. Allow to cool for 10 minutes before transferring to a wire cooling rack.

SUGAR COOKIES

MAKES 24 COOKIES

Sweet sugar cookies with a slight crunch on the outside and soft center that just melt in your mouth—is there anything better? These simple sugar cookies are an age-old recipe that has been passed down to me. This is one of the easiest and most universally loved recipes.

---

1 cup (2 sticks; 8 ounces) unsalted butter, at room temperature
¾ cup powdered sugar
½ cup cornstarch
1¼ cups all-purpose flour
¼ cup sanding sugar (see note)

NOTE

These can be made with different colored sanding sugars, or natural sanding sugar.

---

1. Preheat the oven to 350°F. Line two baking sheets with silicone baking mats or parchment paper.

2. In a large bowl, using a hand (or stand) mixer, cream the butter until fluffy, about 1 minute, then scrape down the sides of the bowl with a spatula.

3. Add the powdered sugar and beat until combined, then scrape down the sides of the bowl. Pour in the cornstarch and flour and, with a spatula or spoon, gently stir until everything is combined (it might seem like the dough is a little too crumbly; it should be soft to the touch).

4. Place the sanding sugar in a shallow bowl.

5. With a 1-tablespoon cookie scoop, scoop a dough ball into the sanding sugar. Gently roll the dough ball so that it gets totally covered in sugar, then place on the prepared baking sheet. Repeat to form all the cookies, placing them about an inch apart.

6. Bake for 10 to 12 minutes and remove from the oven. Allow to cool on the pans for 5 minutes, then transfer to a wire cooling rack to cool and enjoy.

COCONUT CHOCOLATE BARS

Butter
Shredded Coconut
Heavy Cream
Chocolate Chips

MAKES 16 BARS

Coconut makes everything seem tropical and luxurious. A toasted coconut crust and a rich chocolate filling make for one delicious dessert.

---

3 tablespoons unsalted butter, at room temperature, cut into tablespoon-size pieces, plus ½ teaspoon for baking pan
2 cups sweetened shredded coconut
1 cup heavy cream
1 cup semisweet chocolate chips

1. Preheat the oven to 350°F. Grease an 8-inch square baking pan with the ½ teaspoon of butter and set aside.

2. In a food processor, process the 3 tablespoons of butter and the coconut on high speed for 1 minute. Pour into the prepared baking pan and press down to form a crust on the bottom. Bake for 18 to 20 minutes, or until the edges start to brown.

3. Remove from the oven and set aside.

4. In a small pot, bring the cream to a boil, 5 minutes. Remove from the heat and pour in the chocolate chips. With a spatula, stir well until combined, 2 minutes, then pour the mixture over the coconut crust. Allow to cool in the refrigerator for an hour (or overnight) until set. When ready to serve, cut into bars and enjoy.

JAM CRUMB BARS

MAKES 32 BARS

These bars are my jam (pun intended!). They are my favorite dessert when I need to feed a crowd. Around the holidays or during the summers I find myself making these bars frequently; they've become a family favorite. What I love about this recipe is that there's no need to scale up a dessert recipe and wonder whether it will make enough for a crowd.

1½ cups (3 sticks; 12 ounces) unsalted butter, divided
2 cups all-purpose flour, divided
1 cup sugar, divided
1 cup rolled oats, divided
2 cups jam (flavor of choice; I usually like to use raspberry or a berry fruit spread)

NOTE

I use a pizza cutter to cut the bars; it works like a charm.

1. Preheat the oven to 375°F. Use a little of the butter to grease a 10 x 15 x 1-inch jelly-roll pan.

2. Cut 1 cup (2 sticks; 8 ounces) of the butter into pieces and place in a food processor. Add 1⅔ cups of the flour, ⅔ cup of the sugar, and ⅓ cup of the oats and process on high speed until combined into a mealy mixture, about 15 seconds.

3. Pour the mixture onto the prepared jelly-roll pan and press down the crumbs to form an even crust.

4. Spread the jam evenly over the crust.

5. In the food processor, combine the remaining scant ½ cup of butter, ⅓ cup of flour, ⅓ cup of sugar, and ⅔ cup of oats and process on high speed until combined, 10 seconds, then spoon the mixture over the jam layer.

6. Bake for 25 minutes, or until the edges are golden brown. Remove from the oven and allow to cool in the pan before cutting into squares. I run a knife around the edges and then cut 32 squares (see note), but you could definitely cut them into even smaller squares to feed an even bigger crowd.

TOFFEE BARS

Butter
Graham Crackers
Brown Sugar
Chocolate Chips

MAKES 36 SMALL SQUARES TOFFEE

This recipe is from my husband's grandmother and is a family favorite around the holidays. During our first Christmas together I learned that my in-laws go all out when making holiday cookie platters—everyone is assigned a recipe and they all get together and have cookie-making parties, it is really something special. These toffee bars were my husband's contribution and immediately upon seeing the handwritten recipe dated 1984, I knew they were going to be good. I was surprised at how easy they were to make and by the simplicity of the recipe—only four ingredients. Now we make them every year around the holidays and they're always a huge hit. They also are great for gifting.

---

1 cup (2 sticks; 8 ounces) unsalted butter, plus more for pan
8 graham cracker cookies
1 cup light brown sugar
1½ cups semisweet chocolate chips

NOTE
Make sure to butter the pan and line with graham crackers before starting to make the toffee part of these bars because that step goes pretty quickly and is hands-on.

1. Butter a 9 x 13-inch baking pan and line the bottom with the graham crackers (see note).

2. In a medium saucepan over medium-high heat, melt the butter and brown sugar together. Bring the mixture to a boil while whisking constantly. Once it reaches a boil, let it remain at a boil for 2 to 3 minutes while whisking constantly.

3. Carefully pour the mixture over the graham crackers and let sit for 5 to 10 minutes.

4. Preheat the oven to 350°F. Put the cracker–lined baking pan in the oven and bake for 10 minutes.

5. Remove from the oven and sprinkle the chocolate chips over the top of the toffee. Put the baking pan back in the oven for 1 minute to melt the chips. Remove from the oven and smooth the chocolate chips over the toffee by running a spatula over them, moving back and forth. Let cool completely and cut into little bars and enjoy.

TUXEDO CASHEW TURTLE CUPS

MAKES 16 TURTLE CUPS (RECIPE EASILY DOUBLES)

These turtle cups are perfect for last-minute holiday parties or when you need to bring something and don't have a bazillion hours to make a dessert (or for when you just don't feel like baking).

½ cup roasted and lightly salted cashews

1 ounce caramel squares (12 to 15 squares), melted

2¾ ounces semisweet baking chocolate, or a heaping ⅓ cup semisweet chocolate chips

2¼ ounces white baking chocolate, or about ⅓ cup white chocolate chips, melted

1 tablespoon sea salt

1. Line a mini muffin pan with 16 mini muffin liners and put three cashews in the bottom of each liner.

2. Place the caramels, semisweet chocolate, and white chocolate in separate microwave-safe bowls and microwave for 30 seconds on HIGH. Remove from the microwave and stir. If an ingredient is not smooth and completely melted, return it to the microwave and microwave for another 10 seconds, then stir again and see whether you need to microwave any more.

3. Spoon a little bit of the melted caramel over the cashews into the cups.

4. Spoon a little bit of semisweet chocolate on one-half of the cup, on top of the caramel and cashews. Spoon a little bit of white chocolate on the other side of the cup (it's okay if they don't touch).

5. Now, gently shake the pan back and forth so that the chocolates settle and touch each other.

6. Sprinkle with the sea salt.

7. Put in the freezer for 30 minutes for fast cooling, or let harden in the refrigerator or even on the counter if you have more time.

CHOCOLATE CHEESECAKE CUPS

Chocolate
Cream Cheese
Sugar
Sour Cream
Egg

MAKES 12 MINI CUPS

What could possibly be better than cheesecake? Why, mini chocolate cheesecake cups, of course. These are a favorite, especially for family dinner desserts—have one cup or two; they're mini so it's totally acceptable to reach for seconds. Although they have a slightly longer baking time then other desserts, they are worth it.

1 ounce (1 square) semisweet baking chocolate (I use Baker's brand), plus ½ square for topping
4 ounces cream cheese, softened
¼ cup sugar
¼ cup sour cream
1 large egg

NOTE
Letting the cheesecake bites bake at a low temperature and keeping them in the oven prevents them from cracking.

1. Preheat the oven to 225°F. Line a mini muffin pan with 12 mini cups or mini muffin liners.

2. Start by placing the 1 ounce of chocolate in a microwave-safe bowl. Microwave for 30 second on HIGH, then remove from the microwave and stir. Repeat, microwaving for 30 seconds and stirring, until the chocolate has melted (mine takes 1½ minutes, or three intervals of heating).

3. In a bowl, using a hand mixer, beat the cream cheese and sugar, then add the sour cream and beat until smooth.

4. With a spoon, fold in the egg (always folding under) and the melted chocolate and stir until smooth.

5. Using a cookie scoop or spoon, scoop 2 tablespoons of the mixture into each cup. Bake for 50 minutes, then turn off the oven and let the chocolate cheesecakes sit in the oven for 30 minutes (see note). Remove from the oven and allow to cool completely before serving (2 hours or overnight in the refrigerator).

6. Shave the remaining chocolate and sprinkle over the cups before serving.

CHOCOLATE PEANUT BUTTER SWIRL FUDGE

MAKES 24 PIECES

Walking down the main street of a small town on a leisurely weekend getaway, chances are you're going to come across a fudge shop. I always love stopping in and seeing all the different flavors. But did you know that you don't have to wait to go to a fudge shop to have incredible fudge? You can make it at home in mere minutes. This recipe is rich and chocolaty and has a delicious peanut butter swirl (see note).

½ cup creamy peanut butter
2 tablespoons powdered sugar
2 cups good-quality semisweet chocolate chips
1 (14-ounce) can sweetened condensed milk

NOTE

If you don't like peanut butter, you can make plain chocolate fudge without the peanut butter swirl.

---

1. Line an 8-inch square baking pan with parchment paper, leaving an overhang on two sides to aid in lifting out later, and set aside.

2. In a small, microwave-safe bowl, microwave the peanut butter for 30 seconds on HIGH, remove from the microwave, stir in powdered sugar, and set aside.

3. Place the chocolate chips in a medium-large, microwave-safe bowl and pour the condensed milk over them (it's okay if the entire can is not emptied; no need to scrape the can contents out). Microwave for 30 seconds on HIGH. Remove from the microwave and stir. Repeat, microwaving for 30 seconds and stirring, until the chips are completely melted (1 minute, or two intervals of heating; microwave for another 10 seconds if everything is not melted).

4. The mixture will start to thicken pretty quickly, so as soon as it is all stirred together, spread it into the prepared baking pan, spoon the peanut butter mixture on top of the chocolate and, with a spatula or butter knife, swirl the peanut butter mixture into the chocolate.

5. Put the fudge in the freezer for 30 minutes (or in the fridge for an hour) and remove it from the freezer. Remove the fudge from the pan by lifting the parchment paper by its edges. Cut the fudge square into three rows and each row into eight pieces.

6. Serve and enjoy or place in the refrigerator for storage.

FROZEN BANANAS FOSTER

Bananas
Vanilla Ice Cream
Milk
Bourbon
Caramel Sauce

SERVES 2 OR 3
(DEPENDING ON HOW BIG YOUR GLASSES ARE)

Bananas Foster is an old-timey dessert, typically made of bananas on top of vanilla ice cream with a caramel sauce, and then alcohol is added and it's ignited. It's quite the spectacle. While loving the flavors, I do not love the amount of preparation it must take to prepare such a dessert, so I made it into this delicious shake, a Frozen Bananas Foster that is oh so delicious.

2 bananas
1 cup vanilla ice cream
1 cup milk
4 ounces bourbon (see note)
1 cup ice cubes
¼ cup caramel sauce

NOTE
This can easily be made into a "mocktail" by omitting the bourbon.

1. Combine the bananas, ice cream, milk, bourbon, and ice cubes in a blender and blend until smooth, about 1 minute.

2. Spoon the caramel sauce around the inside rim of two or three glasses, allowing it to drip down the insides of each glass. Pour the mixture from the blender into the prepared glasses and enjoy.

White Bread
Egg
Milk
Sugar
Rolo Chocolate
Caramel Candy

CHOCOLATE CARAMEL BREAD PUDDING

MAKES 1 INDIVIDUAL CUP

Whenever there is bread pudding on a menu for dessert, my husband will order it. Before stealing little bites of his dessert here and there, I had never given bread pudding a second thought. Not anymore, though, now I absolutely love bread pudding as a dessert and I especially love when they're in little cups. These bread pudding cups are a great dessert for a date night and you'll be pleasantly surprised by how easy they are to make. This recipe is for one cup; you can easily scale the recipe up or down for as many individual cups as you desire (see note).

1 slice fresh or day-old white
   bread
1 large egg
3 tablespoons milk
1 tablespoon sugar, plus a
   pinch for topping
5 Rolo chocolate caramel
   candies, chopped, divided

NOTE
*I usually make four ramekins'
worth and then store the remaining two in the refrigerator for
the next day. To reheat, simply
microwave on HIGH for 30 seconds.*

1. Preheat the oven to 350°F. Spray an individual ramekin with cooking spray and set on a foil-lined baking sheet.

2. Cube the bread and set aside.

3. In a bowl, using a fork, whisk together the egg, milk, and sugar, then add about four of the chopped-up Rolo candies.

4. Add the bread cubes and stir to coat the bread with the egg mixture. Pour into the prepared ramekin, top with remaining chopped Rolo bits, and sprinkle a pinch of sugar on top.

5. Place the ramekin on the prepared baking sheet (to catch any drippings) and bake for 30 minutes (it will puff up as it bakes). Remove from the oven. Allow to cool for 10 minutes before serving.

PANNA COTTA AND PEACHES

Unflavored Gelatin
Heavy Cream
Sugar
Vanilla Extract
Peach

SERVES 4 TO 6 (SMALL PORTIONS)

Panna cotta is an incredibly easy dessert to make. It is a cold molded dessert that looks super fancy but is deceptively simple to make and takes no longer than five minutes to prep. The end result is a rich and creamy texture that is complemented perfectly with sweet and tart peach slices (see note).

1½ tablespoons water
1 teaspoon unflavored gelatin
1 cup heavy cream
¼ cup sugar
½ teaspoon vanilla extract
1 peach, pitted and finely
   sliced

NOTES

You can top this dessert with any fruit you desire. Soft fruit works best; think berries or bananas. Unflavored gelatin is found in the baking aisle or next to the powdered gelatin dessert mixes in most grocery stores.

1. In a large bowl, combine the water and gelatin, stir once, and let sit for 4 minutes.

2. While the water and gelatin are coming together, in a microwave-safe bowl, microwave the heavy cream and sugar for 30 seconds on HIGH. Remove from the microwave and stir. Repeat, microwaving for 30 seconds and stirring, for a total of 1½ minutes, or three intervals of heating.

3. Remove the bowl from the microwave and stir in the vanilla, then pour the warm cream mixture over the gelatin mixture. Stir and make sure that all the gelatin and sugar have dissolved, then pour into four to six little bowls or cups. Cover with plastic wrap and let set in the refrigerator for 2 hours (or overnight).

4. When ready to serve, remove the plastic wrap and place little peach slices on top of the panna cotta.

PEANUT BUTTER POPCORN

**MAKES 7 CUPS POPCORN MIXTURE;
SERVES 12 TO 14 (RECIPE DOUBLES EASILY)**

This peanut butter popcorn is simply irresistible; it is a must-make recipe and is absolutely perfect for parties. A few years ago my husband and I went to a friend's house for a party and the hostess had little bowls of a popcorn mixture sitting out in the center of all the tables. I had some and couldn't stop eating it—it was so good. She shared the recipe with me and I have been making it ever since, adding Reese's peanut butter cups because they make life better, don't they? This popcorn mixture is sweet and crunchy and addictively delicious.

4 Reese's peanut butter cups,
　cut into small pieces
5 cups popped popcorn
1½ cups crispy rice cereal
1¼ cups white chocolate
　chips, melted
2 tablespoons creamy peanut
　butter, melted

1. Line a baking sheet with parchment paper and set aside.

2. Put the chopped peanut butter cups, popped popcorn, and cereal in a large bowl (if you don't have a bowl large enough, evenly distribute the ingredients into two bowls) and stir with a wooden spoon.

3. In a microwave-safe bowl, microwave the white chocolate and peanut butter for 30 seconds on HIGH. Then remove from the microwave and stir. Repeat, microwaving for 30 seconds and stirring, for a total of 1 minute, or two intervals of heating. Pour over the popcorn mixture and stir.

4. Pour the popcorn mixture onto the prepared baking sheet and let it cool for about 1 hour, or until it has set, then break it up into chunks and serve.

TRAIL MIX

**MAKES 3½ CUPS TRAIL MIX,
OR ABOUT 14 (¼-CUP) SERVINGS**

Peanuts
M&M's
Raisins
Chocolate Chips
Pecans

Trail mix is one of my favorite snacks to have on hand. It's a great snack for when you're on the go or you have guests and want to put out a little bowl of treats for everyone to enjoy as you make a meal.

1¾ cups lightly salted, dry-roasted peanuts
½ cup M&M's
½ cup raisins
¼ cup semisweet chocolate chips
½ cup pecan halves

1. Combine all the ingredients in a large bowl and stir.
2. Store in an airtight container or sealable storage bag.

GINGERSNAP PEACH CRUMBLE

SERVES 4 TO 6

This is one of the easiest desserts to make and it is so delicious. Fresh peaches are topped with gingersnap cookie crumbles and are baked to perfection. This makes for a great dessert on summer nights when you have last-minute guests or are looking for a sweet treat but are short on time.

---

6 peaches, pitted and sliced (see notes)

20 to 24 gingersnap cookies, crushed (I like Nabisco brand)

4 tablespoons unsalted butter, cut into 4 pieces

NOTE

Instead of fresh peaches you can use canned peaches, just drain the liquid off. This crumble goes great with a scoop of vanilla ice cream on top (see page 224 for a homemade recipe).

---

1. Preheat the oven to 400°F.
2. Place the peach slices in the bottom of a pie dish or baking dish.
3. In a food processor, process the cookies for 3 seconds, then add the butter pieces and process for 3 seconds, or until a crumbly mixture forms.
4. Sprinkle the gingersnap cookie crumbles over the peaches.
5. Bake for 20 minutes. Remove from the oven, allow to cool for a few minutes, and then serve.

BANANA CARAMEL CREAM PIE

Bananas
Heavy Cream
Sugar
Graham Cracker Piecrust
Caramel Sauce

MAKES 1 PIE; SERVES 8

Make this pie once and you'll want to make it over and over again—and you'll get requests to do so. It's so easy to make and requires no baking. This pie happens to be my husband's favorite dessert and I always feel like I'm keeping a secret by how simple it is. The next time you're in need of a dessert that takes all of five minutes to make, look no further than this recipe.

3 ripe bananas
1 cup heavy cream
2 tablespoons sugar
1 premade (9-inch) graham cracker piecrust
3 tablespoons caramel sauce

NOTE
Store the pie in the refrigerator. This pie also freezes really well and becomes a frozen ice cream–like pie, so that is a serving option.

1. In a bowl, mash the bananas and set aside.

2. In another bowl, combine the cream and sugar and beat with a hand (or stand) mixer for 3 minutes, or until soft peaks form (don't overbeat; you want the cream to come together and be able to hold its shape when a spoon is run through it).

3. Add the bananas and beat for another 30 seconds.

4. Spoon the mixture into the graham cracker piecrust and drizzle the caramel sauce on top. Serve immediately or store in the refrigerator until you are ready to serve it (see note).

NO-BAKE WHITE CHOCOLATE LIME PIE

MAKES 1 PIE; SERVES 8

Super refreshing, this sweet and tart pie will knock your socks off, it's so good. The texture of the pie is silky smooth with zesty lime throughout; it's an all-around crowd-pleaser.

½ cup white chocolate chips
½ cup heavy cream
1 (14-ounce) can sweetened condensed milk
3 limes (1 zested for 1 tablespoon zest and all 3 juiced for ½ cup lime juice)
1 premade (9-inch) graham cracker piecrust

NOTE

If there are any leftovers, this pie can be frozen and served as an ice-cream pie.

1. In a microwave-safe bowl, microwave the white chocolate for 30 seconds on HIGH. Then remove from the microwave and stir. Repeat, microwaving for 30 seconds and stirring, for a total of 1 minute, or two intervals of heating. If not smooth and creamy, microwave for another 15 seconds, stir, and set aside.

2. In another bowl, beat the cream with a hand mixer until soft peaks form, 2 minutes at medium speed. Slowly pour in the sweetened condensed milk and beat until combined, 15 seconds. Slowly add the melted white chocolate and beat until combined, 15 seconds. Add the lime zest and juice and beat again until combined, 15 seconds.

3. Pour into the graham cracker piecrust and refrigerate for an hour (or overnight), until set, then slice and enjoy.

S'MORES SWIRL PIE

Graham Cracker Piecrust

Eggs

Chocolate

Butter

Marshmallow Crème

SERVES 8

This pie is super decadent and rich, reminiscent of time spent around a campfire, but—dare I say—so much tastier than regular ol' s'mores. And in pie form, it is begging to be brought to parties.

1 premade (9-inch) graham cracker piecrust

3 large eggs

8 ounces semisweet baking chocolate, roughly chopped, or 1½ cups semisweet chocolate chips

4 tablespoons unsalted butter, cut into 4 pieces

1 (7-ounce) jar marshmallow crème

1. Preheat the oven to 325°F. Place the graham cracker piecrust on a baking sheet and set aside.

2. With a hand (or stand) mixer, beat the eggs until they have doubled in size, around 3 minutes.

3. In a microwave-safe bowl, combine the chocolate and butter and microwave for 30 seconds on HIGH. Remove from the microwave and stir. Repeat, microwaving for 30 seconds and stirring, until the chocolate and butter have melted together (a total of 1½ minutes, or three intervals of heating).

4. Using a spatula, gently fold half of the egg mixture into the chocolate mixture (always folding underneath to over) until combined, then fold in the remaining egg mixture. With the spatula, spoon the batter into the graham cracker crust.

5. With a butter knife, spread the marshmallow crème on top of the chocolate batter in the center and swirl it so that some chocolate batter mixes with the marshmallow crème. Bake the pie for 35 to 40 minutes, until the pie filling has puffed up. Remove from the oven and allow it to rest for at least 30 minutes before serving (the top will deflate). I like to let the pie cool and then refrigerate it overnight—it has a great, almost fudgelike consistency that way.

ICEBOX CAKE

Cream Cheese
Sugar
Cool Whipped Topping
Nutella
Chocolate Graham Crackers

SERVES 8

I'm such a huge fan of no-bake desserts and Nutella that it is no wonder I'm totally crazy about this recipe. When it all comes together, your guests are guaranteed to love the result.

---

1 (8-ounce) package cream cheese, softened
½ cup sugar
6 ounces cool whipped topping, at room temperature
⅔ cup Nutella
20 chocolate graham cracker rectangles (see notes)

NOTES
You can use any flavor of graham crackers for this; I've used cinnamon or honey and the results are always amazing with the hazelnut chocolate filling. If you don't have time to let it set in the refrigerator, you can freeze it for an hour. Then store the cake in the refrigerator.

---

1. In a bowl, with a hand (or stand) mixer, beat together the cream cheese and sugar until light and fluffy, about 2 minutes. Scrape the sides of the bowl with a spatula and add the cool whipped topping. Beat until smooth, about 1 minute. Transfer half of the cheese mixture to another bowl.

2. Add the Nutella to one of the bowls of cream cheese and beat until combined, about 1 minute.

3. Lay out four pieces of plastic wrap (cut each piece to 1½ to 2 feet long) and crisscross them, alternating them lengthwise and widthwise.

4. Lay down four graham cracker rectangles next to each other—the long sides of the graham crackers should be touching—in the center of the top layer of plastic wrap.

5. Spread half of the Nutella-free cream cheese mixture onto the graham crackers. Place four graham cracker rectangles on top of the cream cheese mixture.

6. Spread half of the Nutella mixture onto the graham crackers. Place four graham cracker rectangles on top of the Nutella mixture and press down lightly, lining up the corners as you're working.

7. Spread the remaining Nutella-free cheese mixture onto the graham crackers. Place four graham cracker rectangles on top of the cream cheese mixture.

8. Spread the remaining Nutella mixture onto the graham crackers. Place the remaining four graham cracker rectangles on top of the Nutella mixture and press down lightly.

9. Gently press down to make sure you have formed a rectangle whose corners align. Wrap the plastic wrap around the rectangle (the "cake") and refrigerate it for 2 hours or overnight (see notes). To serve, remove the plastic and, with a sharp knife, carefully cut into slices. Serve and enjoy. Store in the refrigerator.

ORANGE CHOCOLATE ALMOND TORTE

Eggs
Sugar
Almond Meal
Orange
Chocolate Chips

SERVES 8

This delicate torte is almost like a sponge cake. It's super light, but at the same time it is rich and flavorful. A torte is typically a cake made with little to no flour. Until one of my best friends told me this, I had always thought tortes were just another name for superfancy cakes. Now, whenever I make tortes, I carry the feeling of being fancy, while actually knowing the definition.

5 large eggs, whites and yolks divided
1 cup sugar
2 cups almond meal (see notes)
Zest and juice of 1 orange (should be about 1 tablespoon of zest)
½ cup semisweet chocolate chips

NOTES
Almond meal can be found in most major grocery stores, in the baking or gluten-free aisle. The key to this light and fluffy cake is the beaten egg whites. I always start by beating the egg whites; that way I know that step is done right. If you get anything in the egg whites (such as some yolk parts or sugar), they will not form the desired peaks.

1. Preheat the oven to 350°F. Line a springform pan with parchment paper and spray with cooking spray.

2. With a hand (or stand) mixer, beat the egg whites until soft peaks form, about 3 minutes (see notes). In another bowl beat the egg yolks until creamy in color, 1 minute, then slowly add the sugar and beat until the mixture thickens slightly, 1 minute. Add the almond meal, the orange zest, and 2 tablespoons of the orange juice and beat until combined, 1 minute.

3. With a spatula, fold one-third of the egg whites into the almond flour mixture (always folding under). When incorporated, fold another third of the egg whites into the almond flour mixture, and then the remaining third of egg whites should be folded in.

4. Pour the batter into the prepared springform pan and bake for 30 minutes, or until a toothpick comes out clean (the center may look a little jiggly still, but the toothpick should come out clean). Remove from the oven and allow the cake to cool. Gently run a butter knife around the edges of the cake and remove the springform pan. Place the cake on a plate.

5. Microwave the chocolate chips in a microwave-safe bowl for 30 seconds on HIGH, stir, then microwave in 30-second intervals, stirring in between until the chocolate has melted (mine usually takes 2 minutes, or 4 intervals of heating). Pour the chocolate over the top of the cake and allow it to cool (it will harden). Cut the torte into slices and enjoy.

STRAWBERRIES AND CREAM TARTLETS

MAKES 6 MINI TARTLETS

When you're looking for a quick dessert and don't feel like using your oven, look no further than these tartlets. They're adorable and conjure up memories of childhood and summertime. Just imagine coming inside after a day of being out in the hot sun and enjoying one of these cold mini desserts. They're creamy and fruity and crave-worthy.

---

6 mini graham cracker piecrusts

½ pint strawberries, hulled and sliced (½ to ¾ cup sliced)

⅓ cup plus 1 teaspoon sugar

8 ounces reduced-fat cream cheese, softened (see note)

8 ounces cool whipped topping, at room temperature (see note)

NOTE

To get the cream cheese and cool whipped topping to room temperature, I simply put them out on the counter 30 minutes to an hour before making this recipe.

---

1. Set mini piecrusts on a plate or baking sheet.

2. Place the sliced strawberries in a bowl and sprinkle with 1 teaspoon of the sugar, stir once or twice until the strawberries are coated, and set aside.

3. In a large bowl, with a hand (or stand) mixer, beat the cream cheese and remaining ⅓ cup of sugar until smooth and creamy, then add the cool whipped topping and beat until combined. The mixture will be thick.

4. With a spatula, scoop a sixth of the filling and press it into one of the mini piecrusts. Repeat until all of the mini pies are filled. Top each filled tartlet with a few strawberries and refrigerate on their plate or baking sheet to set, about 1 hour or overnight, then store them in the refrigerator. (Alternatively you can store them in the freezer and serve frozen as ice-cream tartlets.)

VANILLA POUND CAKE

Butter
Sugar
Vanilla Extract
Eggs
Flour

MAKES 1 POUND CAKE, ABOUT 12 SLICES

Whoever said vanilla was boring clearly never had this pound cake. Made with Madagascar vanilla extract, this cake is simply delicious; it is perfect for any occasion, at any time of the year. You'll be so impressed by how easy it is to make.

1 cup (2 sticks; 8 ounces) unsalted butter, at room temperature
1½ cups sugar
1 tablespoon Madagascar vanilla extract (see notes)
4 large eggs
1¾ cups all-purpose flour
¼ teaspoon salt

NOTES

Because you want vanilla flavor to really come through, I would recommend using a high-quality vanilla extract. You can really take this pound cake to the next level by adding seasonal berries to it as a topping (in the summer, think freshly sliced strawberries; in the winter, think adding some cranberries or frozen berries).

1. Preheat the oven to 325°F. Grease an 8½ x 4½ x 2¾-inch loaf pan with butter or cooking spray and set aside.

2. In a large bowl, with a hand (or stand) mixer, cream the butter and sugar until fluffy, about 2 minutes. Scrape down the sides of the bowl with a spatula, then add the vanilla and eggs and beat until combined.

3. Slowly add the flour and salt and beat on low speed until combined.

4. Pour the batter into the prepared loaf pan and bake for 50 to 60 minutes, or until a toothpick inserted into the center comes out clean. Allow to cool in the pan, then remove from the pan, slice, and serve.

HOMEMADE SAUCES/SPICE MIXES/EXTRAS

ALFREDO SAUCE

Butter
Garlic
Heavy Cream
Yogurt
Parmesan Cheese

MAKES ABOUT 2 CUPS SAUCE

Creamy, rich, and oh so delicious—this is my favorite sauce for topping pasta (or anything, really, because it is seriously addicting). My version of Alfredo sauce has a little yogurt in it, which really rounds out the flavor. It turns out perfectly every time.

½ cup (1 stick; 4 ounces) salted or unsalted butter
1 garlic clove, pressed
1 cup heavy cream
⅓ cup plain yogurt
½ teaspoon salt
1½ cups (5 ounces) shredded Parmesan cheese

1. In a medium saucepan over high heat, melt the butter, about 3 minutes.

2. Add the garlic, cream, yogurt, and salt and whisk until the mixture comes to a slow boil, 5 minutes. Lower the heat to medium, add the cheese, and whisk for 2 minutes, or until the cheese has melted.

3. Cook over low heat for 5 minutes, remove from the heat, and serve.

PESTO

MAKES 1½ CUPS PESTO

In this recipe, pine nuts are toasted to perfection before being combined with fresh basil to make a delicious pesto sauce. Pesto can be used on pasta as a sauce, on salads as a dressing, or on sandwiches as a spread and always reminds me of bright summer days when the herb garden is in its full glory.

½ cup pine nuts (see notes)
2 cups fresh basil
¼ cup shredded Parmesan cheese
1 garlic clove, halved
½ teaspoon salt
⅓ cup extra-virgin olive oil

NOTES

If you don't like pine nuts, you could substitute walnuts. If I have leftover pesto, I freeze it: I simply put 3 to 4 tablespoons of pesto in a small storage container (you could even use an ice cube tray as a mold, and then you'd have frozen cubes of pesto), and when I'm ready to use it, I let it thaw in the refrigerator.

1. Preheat the oven to 350°F. Line a baking sheet with aluminum foil and place the pine nuts on the baking sheet. Bake for 5 minutes, or until slightly golden brown and fragrant.

2. Place the pine nuts, basil, cheese, garlic clove halves, and salt in a food processor and pulsate for 5 seconds, then slowly drizzle in the olive oil and process for 10 seconds. Scrape down the sides with a spatula, and if you see any larger pieces remaining, pulsate for another few seconds. Store in an airtight container in the refrigerator for up to a week, or freeze the leftovers (see notes).

SPICE MIXES

My spice cabinet is out of control. I have so many spices because I really love different seasoning combinations and how they can transform the flavor of a dish. I once ran out of a favorite spice blend and decided to make it myself and loved the result, so here are three of my very favorite spice blend recipes:

MEDITERRANEAN-SPICED SEA SALT

MAKES 3½ TABLESPOONS SALT BLEND

1 tablespoon dried oregano
1½ teaspoons garlic powder
1 teaspoon dried thyme
1 teaspoon salt

½ teaspoon dried basil
½ teaspoon lemon pepper or freshly ground
  black pepper

TACO SEASONING/MEXICAN-SPICE BLEND

MAKES ABOUT 2½ TABLESPOONS SEASONING

1 tablespoon chili powder
1½ teaspoons cumin
1 teaspoon salt
½ teaspoon garlic powder

½ teaspoon paprika
½ teaspoon freshly ground black pepper
¼ teaspoon dried oregano

ITALIAN SEASONING

MAKES ABOUT 3 TABLESPOONS SEASONING

1 tablespoon dried basil
1 tablespoon dried parsley
1 teaspoon garlic powder

½ teaspoon dried thyme
½ teaspoon dried rosemary
¼ teaspoon freshly ground black pepper

QUICK KETCHUP

Tomatoes
Brown Sugar
Cider Vinegar
Paprika
Worcestershire Sauce

MAKES 1 CUP KETCHUP

My recipe for quick ketchup came about out of necessity: I was out of ketchup. I decided I'd try to make my own and was so impressed by how good it tasted and how easy it was to make, now I'm hooked on this quick ketchup recipe.

---

1 cup cut-up tomatoes (see notes)
2 tablespoons light brown sugar
2 teaspoons cider vinegar
1½ teaspoons salt (see notes)
1 teaspoon paprika
1 teaspoon Worcestershire sauce

NOTES
I like to use two big tomatoes and a handful of cherry tomatoes, but three big tomatoes does the trick, too. I only slightly core the tomatoes so there are a few seeds that still remain. If you want a more seed-free ketchup, cut the tomatoes and remove the seeds before cooking. If you don't like ketchups with a slightly sweet taste, add a little extra salt.

1. Core and quarter any big tomatoes.
2. Put all the ingredients into a medium saucepan. Bring to a boil, stirring occasionally.
3. When the mixture comes to a boil, lower the heat to medium and let the mixture slowly boil for 10 minutes.
4. Remove from the heat and allow to cool for 5 minutes, then put into either a blender or a food processor and process until smooth in consistency, about 1 minute. Transfer to a container and serve. This ketchup is best served after letting it cool in the refrigerator for a few hours.
5. Refrigerate for storage; lasts up to 4 weeks in an airtight container.

QUICK MARINARA SAUCE

Olive Oil
Onion
Garlic
Tomatoes
Tomato Paste

MAKES ABOUT 2 HEAPING CUPS MARINARA
PERFECT FOR 1 POUND OF PASTA

In the summer I grow tomatoes and love making this sauce with fresh ones. It comes together in under half an hour and is the perfect homemade alternative to store-bought marinara sauce.

2 tablespoons extra-virgin olive oil
1 small onion, finely chopped
1 garlic clove, pressed
2 pounds fresh tomatoes, chopped (about 6 large tomatoes)
2 tablespoons tomato paste
1 teaspoon salt
¼ teaspoon freshly ground black pepper

NOTE

If I have leftover marinara sauce, I freeze it; it keeps frozen for up to 3 months.

1. In a large pot with a lid over medium heat, heat the olive oil for 1 minute, then add the onion and cook for 3 minutes, stirring occasionally. Add the garlic and sauté for another 2 minutes, and add the tomatoes and tomato paste. Sprinkle with the salt and pepper. Bring to a boil, lower the heat to low, cover, and simmer for 20 minutes.

2. Allow to cool slightly, pour into a food processor, and process for 10 seconds (pulsate for a few additional seconds if there are still any chunks remaining). Use immediately or store in an airtight container in the refrigerator; the sauce will last for up to 2 weeks in the refrigerator (see note).

RESTAURANT-STYLE SALSA

MAKES ABOUT 2 HEAPING CUPS SALSA

I'm pretty sure I could live off chips and salsa. And not just any salsa. This salsa will transport you to a Mexican restaurant where perhaps there's constant chip and salsa refills. Those are the best kind of restaurants, right? By the time the meal comes, I am never even hungry—I'm just content from the chips and salsa. I set out to re-create that salsa at home and have to say that this recipe is exactly what the title says: restaurant-style salsa. It's super easy and super amazing.

2 (14.5-ounce) cans diced tomatoes, drained (see notes)
¼ cup fresh cilantro
½ medium red onion
2 garlic cloves
1 jalapeño pepper (see notes)
1 teaspoon salt

1. Place all the ingredients in a food processor (see notes) and process for 15 seconds. Scrape down the sides and process for another 5 seconds. Pour into a bowl or storage container and refrigerate for 1 hour (or overnight). Alternatively, you can put the salsa in the freezer for 10 minutes, then enjoy.

NOTES
Instead of plain diced tomatoes, you could mix up the flavors by adding diced tomatoes with chiles or other flavors. Depending on how spicy you like your salsa, you could use half the amount of jalapeño or double; it's all about your spice level preference: With one jalapeño, the salsa is medium spicy. If you don't have a food processor, you can chop all the ingredients and make it into a pico de gallo (a fresh chopped salsa).

EASY PIECRUST

Flour
Sugar
Butter

MAKES 1 (9-INCH) SINGLE PIECRUST

Homemade piecrust is easy to make. Yes, you read that right: Piecrust is easy to make. The trick to making the best piecrust is to use your food processor. In a few simple steps, you'll have a piecrust begging to be filled.

1¼ cups all-purpose flour,
   plus more for rolling
½ cup sugar
¼ teaspoon salt
½ cup (1 stick; 4 ounces)
   unsalted cold butter,
   cut into 1-inch pieces
   (see notes)
2 tablespoons to ¼ cup ice
   water (see notes)

NOTES

A key to good piecrust is making sure all the ingredients stay cold. I always cut the butter and put it in the freezer for a few minutes to ensure I didn't accidentally heat it up when cutting. For the ice water, I measure out 2 tablespoons of water and then put two ice cubes in the measuring cup and let them melt until I'm ready to use the water.

1. Put the flour, sugar, salt, and butter pieces in a food processor. Process for 8 to 10 seconds, or until the mixture resembles a crumbly mixture with some pea-size pieces of butter remaining.

2. With the food processor running, slowly drizzle in 2 tablespoons of the ice water and process for 10 seconds. The dough should come together and not be sticky. If it is crumbly, drizzle in another tablespoon of water and check again; if it still needs more water, add another tablespoon and process and check again. Alternatively, if the mixture is too wet (the dough should not stick to your finger when touched), add a tablespoon of flour.

3. Carefully remove the dough from the food processor and form it into a disk. Wrap in plastic wrap and put in the freezer for 30 minutes.

4. Sprinkle a board with flour, then remove the disk from the freezer and sprinkle with a little flour and roll it out with a rolling pin so that it is a little less than a ¼ inch thick and big enough to fit in a pie dish, 10 to 12 inches in diameter.

5. Drape the dough over your pie pan and crimp the edges, then fill with your desired filling and bake.

VANILLA ICE CREAM

MAKES 3 CUPS ICE CREAM

This recipe should really be called "The BEST Vanilla Ice Cream" because after having this homemade version, you'll forever hold all other vanilla ice creams against this standard. What makes this vanilla so good is that it uses a hint of almond extract. Although you'd never know it's there, it really brings out the vanilla flavor and gives it that extra pizzazz.

---

1 cup milk
¾ cup sugar
Pinch of salt
2 cups heavy cream
2 tablespoons pure vanilla
  extract (see note)
½ teaspoon almond extract

NOTE
Since vanilla extract is the main flavoring in this ice cream, be sure to use a high-quality extract, such as Madagascar vanilla extract.

1. Combine all the ingredients in a medium saucepan and heat over high heat for 2 to 3 minutes, or until the sugar has dissolved. Remove from the heat and allow the mixture to cool for 5 to 10 minutes (I do this by putting the pot in the refrigerator).

2. Once the mixture has cooled down, pour it into your ice-cream maker and follow the manufacturer's directions. Mine say to turn it on and let it go for about 25 minutes.

3. Let the machine do its thing, and as soon as it is thick and creamy, transfer the ice cream to a storage container and store in the freezer.

4. Scoop and enjoy.

MENUS AND SHOPPING LISTS

COUPLES COOKING

Grab your partner, a glass of wine, turn on those slow jams, and cook a meal together for a fun date night in.

Couples cooking can be a really fun activity; you're both learning in the kitchen and making dinner together. Here are my five tips for couples cooking:

1. **Delegate**: Decide who is going to do what. There's nothing worse than stepping on someone's' toes (figuratively and literally, it hurts LOL), so divvy up the dishes and decide who is going to do what. My recommendation is that one person makes the quick appetizer and dessert, while the other person makes the main portion of the meal.

2. **Talk about favorite foods**: I like to build the menu that we're cooking around some of our favorites. For example, I learned that my husband's favorite dessert was banana caramel cream pie, and since that's such an easy dessert to make when we are cooking together, I like to include that on the menu. One of my favorites is green beans, so I love having that as part of the menu as well. It's all about picking dishes that you will both enjoy.

3. **Learn from each other**: Don't know the best way to do something? Ask your partner and figure it out together.

4. **Slow down**: Cooking dinner together isn't a race to get things done; it's an opportunity to spend some quality time together, so slow down and enjoy it!

5. **Keep it fun**: There's no wrong or right way to do couples cooking; do what works for you and have fun.

Couples Cooking Menu

Polenta Pizza Bites, page 67
Crusted Pork Chops and Green Beans, page 129

Banana Caramel Cream Pie, page 197

Couples Cooking Shopping List

FROM THE PANTRY:
Cooking spray
Italian seasoning
Extra-virgin olive oil

Sugar
Salt
Freshly ground black pepper

FROM THE STORE:
1 large tomato
3 ripe bananas
1½ pounds pork chops (4 pork chops)
1 cup shredded low-moisture, part skim
   mozzarella cheese
1 cup heavy cream
1 (18-ounce) tube precooked polenta

Dijon mustard
Caramel sauce
Italian-style panko bread crumbs
1 premade (9-inch) graham cracker piecrust
1 (16-ounce) bag frozen French-style green
   beans

DATE NIGHT IN

I love date nights in. Instead of going out to dinner, you can create a super delicious menu at home. My date night menu includes Red Wine Steak and Mushrooms, the first meal my husband cooked for a date night in, and then I pair that with some Rosemary Garlic Parmesan Frites; it's truly a delicious meal. And don't forget dessert. For this menu I've included S'mores Swirl Pie but really any kind of chocolaty dessert (such as the Brownie Bites, page 16) is perfect for date night.

Date Night In Menu

Red Wine Steak and Mushrooms, page 98
Rosemary Garlic Parmesan Frites, page 76

S'mores Swirl Pie, page 201

Date Night In Shopping List

FROM THE PANTRY:
Salt
Freshly ground black pepper

Vegetable oil
Extra-virgin olive oil

FROM THE STORE:
¾ cup red wine
8 ounces white mushrooms
4 medium to large russet or Idaho potatoes
2 garlic cloves
Fresh rosemary
2 rib-eye steaks (1½ to 2 pounds total)
3 large eggs

6 tablespoons unsalted butter
¼ cup grated Parmesan cheese
1 (7-ounce) jar marshmallow crème
1 premade (9-inch) graham cracker piecrust
8 ounces semisweet chocolate or 1½ cups semi-sweet chocolate chips

FANCY MADE SIMPLE

You don't have to go to a fancy restaurant to have fancy foods, and it doesn't have to be super hard to make fancy foods. One of my best friends Lynn is the epitome of effortless fancy made simple. She is a busy lawyer during the day but still comes home and cooks dinner for her family (she has a blog, orderinthekitchen.com). The meals that are fancy made simple include a whole roasted chicken (it's super easy, trust me) and Panna Cotta and Peaches. Both recipes are great because they only take a short time to prep, then there's a little break as they cook and set, while you can get a few of your home to-do list items checked off, and then come back to an amazing fancy-yet-supersimple-to-make meal and dessert.

Fancy Made Simple Menu

Lemon-Roasted Chicken and Potatoes, page 110   Panna Cotta and Peaches, page 189

Fancy Made Simple Shopping List

FROM THE PANTRY:
Extra-virgin olive oil
Mediterranean-spiced sea salt
Salt

Sugar
Pure vanilla extract

FROM THE STORE:
4 to 6 medium yellow potatoes
1 lemon
1 peach

1 (5- to 8-pound) whole chicken
1 cup heavy cream
Unflavored gelatin

FREEZER MEALS

Freezer meals are fantastic. What I like to do is to make a few freezer meals on the weekend, and then throughout the week I can just go to the freezer and have dinner ready in a flash.

Here are the dishes (and cookies) I love to have on hand in the freezer.

Freezer Meals Menu

Sloppy Joe Sandwiches, page 101
Spinach Alfredo Lasagne, page 153

Stuffed Peppers, page 102
Candy Bar Cheesecake Cookies, page 165

Freezer Meals Shopping List

FROM THE PANTRY:
1 cup all-purpose flour
Freshly ground black pepper

Salt
¾ cup sugar

FROM THE STORE:
4 bell peppers
1 red onion
2 pounds lean ground beef
½ cup (1 stick; 4 ounces) unsalted butter
4 ounces cream cheese
1 (15-ounce) container part-skim ricotta cheese
1 cup shredded marble jack cheese
2 cups Italian blend shredded cheese
8 slices pepper jack cheese
1 cup sun-dried tomato Alfredo sauce or marinara sauce

1 (15-ounce) jar creamy Alfredo sauce
1 (9-ounce) package oven-ready lasagna noodles
1 (8.5-ounce) microwave packet whole-grain medley, brown and wild rice
1 (10.75-ounce) can condensed tomato soup, Campbell's preferred
8 wheat hamburger buns (any soft bun would work)
4 Snickers candy bars
1 (24-ounce) package frozen chopped spinach

FAMILY DINNER

Family dinners are a great way to reconnect with your family and share a meal. I was lucky enough to have grown up with Sunday dinners and now have in-laws who continue the tradition and have a family dinner every Sunday.

For family dinner you want something that everyone will love, and that dish is pot roast—it's universally loved and is so easy to make. Along with the main course I always like to make a fun side and then, of course, a dessert.

If you're having family dinner over a long period of time (say, you're gathered together for a football game), it's never a bad idea to make a quick dip, and what's better than an artichoke dip?

My mother-in-law makes the peanut butter cookies into ice cream sandwiches, so add some vanilla ice cream to your list if you'd like to make ice cream sandwiches.

Here is the menu for a family dinner that includes an appetizer, main meal, side dish, and dessert.

Family Dinner Menu

Hearts of Palm and Artichoke Dip, page 61
Crispy Bacon and Brussel Sprouts Salad,
    page 46

Beef Pot Roast with Vegetables,
    page 94
Peanut Butter Sea Salt Cookies, page 169

Family Dinner Shopping List

FROM THE PANTRY:
Salt
Extra-virgin olive oil
2 cups light brown sugar

Pure vanilla extract
Sea salt

FROM THE STORE:
1½ pounds baby potatoes
1 pound Brussel sprouts
1 pound whole carrots
1 lemon
½ pound bacon
1 (3- to 5-pound) beef chuck roast
2 large eggs
½ cup sour cream

8 ounces package cream cheese
1 cup Italian blend shredded cheese
3 cups beef stock
Pure maple syrup
Dijon mustard
1 cup hearts of palm
12 ounces marinated artichoke hearts
2 cups creamy peanut butter

GAME DAY SNACKS

Gathering around the TV for game day can be stressful in and of itself (based on who you're rooting for); why worry about the snacks on top of that? Whenever my husband tells me the guys are coming over, I make these simple favorites.

Game Day Menu

Loaded Tater Tots, page 72
Pepperoni Pizza Pockets, page 68

Peanut Butter Popcorn, page 190

Game Day Shopping List

1 (32-ounce) package Tater Tots or similar
    product
½ pound bacon
1 cup sliced pepperoni
1 large egg
1 cup sour cream
2 cups Mexican blend shredded cheese
1 cup shredded mozzarella cheese
Creamy peanut butter

1½ cups pizza sauce
1 cup salsa
About 5 cups popped popcorn
1½ cups crispy rice cereal
4 (2-crust) packages premade, prerolled
    piecrust
1¼ cups white chocolate chips
4 Reese's peanut butter cups

STOCKING YOUR KITCHEN FOR FIVE-INGREDIENT COOKING

Diced tomatoes: I use diced tomatoes all the time and love using the ones that have extra flavorings in them. For example, diced tomatoes with chiles or fire-roasted diced tomatoes are two that I always keep in my pantry.

Chicken breast tenders: These are such a time saver, I love buying them. Chicken breast tenders are already sliced and the cooking time on them is super quick.

Eggs: Eggs are a great staple to have on hand. They're super versatile. Add an egg on some pizza and you'll have breakfast pizza, or use them to make French toast casserole. Even a simple fried egg on toast or ramen (page 150) are great and simple meals.

Garlic: Nothing helps add an oomph of flavor like a crushed garlic clove. I always keep a few cloves on hand. They're perfect for making easy marinades for meat and perfect to use when roasting veggies.

Mixed shredded cheese blends (e.g., Mexican or Italian shredded cheese): For those ooey-gooey dips and dishes, shredded cheese is my go-to. Another way to add big flavors with few ingredients is to buy cheese blends. A few of my favorites are Mexican cheese blend and four- (or six-) cheese Italian, and I always keep Parmesan on hand.

Peanut butter: When it comes to peanut butter, I like keeping creamy peanut butter on hand. It's great for making a stir-fry (see Tofu Stir-fry with Peanut Sauce, page 154) or for using in desserts, such as the Peanut Butter Sea Salt Cookies (page 169) or Chocolate Peanut Butter Swirl Fudge (page 182).

Sea salt and spiced sea salt blends (e.g., Mediterranean spiced sea salt, store-bought or homemade, page 216): Sea salt and sea salt blends make flavoring your cooking (or baking) a breeze. I have found that sea salt adds a boldness of flavor and is great for topping desserts (e.g., the Peanut Butter Sea Salt Cookies, page 169).

Sour cream: Smooth and creamy with a hint of tang, sour cream is great in so many dishes, it's great for both sweet and savory recipes and is perfect for having on hand for five-ingredient cooking.

FAVORITE KITCHEN TOOLS

Biscuit cutter: A biscuit cutter is new on my list of favorite kitchen tools. It works great for cutting biscuits (page 21) the same size and also for cutting dough for pizza pockets (page 68), or even as a mold for shaping eggs for breakfast sandwiches (page 26).

Cookie scoop: I was gifted a cookie scoop one year and I have since purchased them in different sizes—they're amazing, they make baking same-size cookies and measuring things the same size so much easier.

Food processor: I use my food processor almost every day. It is perfect for making piecrusts and crushing up nuts or making sauces, pesto, or soups.

Hand mixer: Where would I be without my hand mixer? I have a super-small kitchen, so I love my hand mixer because it doesn't take up a lot of room. It makes life super easy when baking cookies or making anything that needs mixing (think whipped cream, cookies, mashed potatoes, and more).

Knives: Sharp knives are a must for any cook. They make the tedious task of chopping easy-peasy.

Pyrex bowls with lids: I use these bowls both as mixing bowls and to store leftovers in the fridge; they are so versatile and handy and I love that they have a lid.

Silicone baking mats: These are a recent find for me and make cleanup super easy. I use them in place of parchment paper when making anything that would stick to the bottom of a baking sheet.

USEFUL INFORMATION

MEAT INTERNAL TEMPERATURES	
Pork Chops	145° to 160°F
Chicken	165° to 170°F
BEEF DONENESS TEMPERATURES	
Rare	130° to 140°F
Medium	155° to 160°F
Well done	165° to 170°F

CONVERSIONS

1½ teaspoons	½ tablespoon	
3 teaspoons	1 tablespoon	
4 tablespoons	¼ cup	
LIQUID INGREDIENTS		
4 ounces	½ cup	120 ml
8 ounces	1 cup	235 ml
16 ounces	1 pint	475 ml
32 ounces	1 quart	946 ml
64 ounces	½ gallon	1.9 L
128 ounces	1 gallon	3.78 L
SOLID INGREDIENTS		
1 ounce	28 g	
4 ounces	¼ pound	115 g
8 ounces	½ pound	225 g
16 ounces	1 pound	455 g
450	230	

OVEN TEMPERATURES	
°F	°C
250	120
300	150
325	170
350	180
375	190
400	200
425	220
450	230

INDEX

* Italics indicate an illustration.